JOHN M. GOTTMAN, PH.D.,

JULIE SCHWARTZ GOTTMAN, PH.D.,

& JOAN DeCLAIRE

Crown Publishers
New York

Ten Lessons

to Transform

Your

Marriage

America's Love Lab Experts

Share Their Strategies for

Strengthening Your Relationship

Published in the United States by Crown Publishers, an imprint of the Crown Publishing Group, a division of Random House, Inc., New York.
www.crownpublishing.com

Crown is a trademark and the Crown colophon is a registered trademark of Random House, Inc.

Library of Congress Cataloging-in-Publication Data
Gottman, John Mordechai.
Ten lessons to transform your marriage : America's love lab experts share their strategies for strengthening your relationship / John M. Gottman, Julie Schwartz Gottman, and Joan DeClaire.
— 1st ed.
p.   cm.
1. Marriage.   2. Marital conflict.   3. Married people—Psychology.   I. Title: Ten lessons to transform your marriage.   II. Gottman, Julie Schwartz.   III. DeClaire, Joan.   IV. Title.
HQ734.G7133 2006
306.81—dc22

2005019645

ISBN-13: 978-1-4000-5018-5
ISBN-10: 1-4000-5018-9

Printed in the United States of America

DESIGN BY ELINA D. NUDELMAN

10   9   8   7   6   5   4   3   2   1

First Edition

To our parents—Lina and Solomon Gotthelfsman,
and Selma and Marvin Schwartz—
in celebration of their long-lasting marriages

—JMG and JSG

Contents

Contents

Acknowledgments

Special thanks to Catherine Romano and the staff at *Reader's Digest* for their collaboration on "The Love Lab" column, upon which this book is based. Thanks also to Virginia Rutter, who provided screening and logistical support for this effort, and to Sybil Carrere, Alyson Shapiro, Amber Tabares, and Janice Driver for making our laboratory work successful.

We also wish to express our continuing gratitude to the people and organizations that help to fund our marriage and family research. These include Bruce and Jolene McCaw, founders of the Apex Foundation and the Talaris Research Institute; Craig Stewart, president of the Apex Foundation; Dan and Sally Kranzler, founders of the Kirlin Foundation; Ron Rabin, executive director of the Kirlin Foundation; Peter Berliner and the Paul G. Allen Family Foundation; Molly Oliveri of the National Institute of Mental Health (NIMH); and a grant from NIMH titled "Basic Processes in Marriage."

In addition, thanks go to the staff of the Gottman Institute: Etana Dykan, Linda Wright, Venita Ramirez, Stacy Walker, Candace Marshall, and Belinda Gray. With great dedication and commitment, they have supported us to serve more than five thousand couples and to train more than fourteen thousand clinicians.

Joan DeClaire wishes to express thanks to Louise Carnachan, Carla Granat, and Debra Jarvis for their tremendously helpful comments on the manuscript. Her gratitude also goes to Wendy Townsend, Bob Heffernan, and the members of the "Artists' Group"—Nan Burling, Louise Carter, Rebecca Hughes, Wendy Slotboom, and Jan Short Pollard—for their never-ending support and encouragement.

And finally, thanks to all the couples who have so generously volunteered for this and other research projects throughout the years.

From Predicting Divorce to Preventing It:

An Introductory Message from John and Julie Gottman

I t's been more than a decade since John and his colleagues at the University of Washington (UW) first announced their discovery: Through the power of careful observation and mathematical analysis, the team had learned to predict with more than 90 percent accuracy whether a married couple would stay together or eventually divorce.

This discovery captured the imagination of many. If research psychologists could now pinpoint specific behaviors that lead to divorce, then perhaps people in troubled relationships could change those behaviors and save their marriages.But as any weatherman can tell you, the ability to predict trouble is not the same as the ability to prevent it. It's one thing to detect a storm brewing on radar; it's quite another to make those storm clouds disappear.

And yet that's the kind of work we at the Gottman Institute have been doing. Since 1994 we've been developing tools to help couples identify problems that are proven to destroy relationships—and to turn those problems around. By experimenting with various forms of therapy, we've been learning how to help husbands and wives improve their marriages and prevent divorce.

Through our workshops, therapy sessions, and books, couples are gaining the tools they need to build stronger friendships and manage their conflicts. As a result, they are learning to work through a whole host of problems common to marriage—problems such as these:

- *the stress of caring for a new baby*

- *exhaustion from working too hard*

- *loss of interest in sex and romance*

- *health problems*

- *recovering from an extramarital affair*

- *struggles with depression*

- *arguments over housework and finances*

- *changes that come with retirement*

- *the loss of a job, an identity, or a lifelong dream*

And once again we're achieving some exciting results. Our studies show that 86 percent of people who complete our marriage workshops say they make significant progress on conflicts that once felt "gridlocked." And after one year, 75 percent of husbands and 56 percent of wives who attend our workshops and therapy sessions feel their marriages move from a broken state to a functional one. Even simply reading our books can make a difference. One study showed that 63 percent of husbands and wives who read John's 1999 bestseller, *The Seven Principles for Making Marriage Work,* reported that their marriages had changed for the better and were still improved a year later.

These numbers are a big improvement over other forms of marital intervention. For example, acclaimed marriage researcher Neil Jacobson conducted an evaluation of one of the most highly regarded therapy methods and showed that only 35 percent of couples using it improved their marriages.

What's behind our success? We believe it's the science. The tools we've developed—and that you'll see real couples using in this book—aren't based on our beliefs or whims about marriage. They are grounded in decades of work John and his colleagues have been doing at the Family Research Laboratory, originally located at UW and now part of our Relationship Research Institute in Seattle. The Love Lab—as we've come to call it—is a research facility where husbands and wives are screened, interviewed, and observed interacting with each other. Researchers use video cameras, heart monitors, and other biofeedback equipment to determine people's stress levels during conversations with their partners. This information is then coded and mathematically analyzed. By collecting and analyzing such data on thousands of couples—and tracking their progress over time—we've learned an enormous amount about the dynamics of marriage. And, ultimately, we've been able to determine which interactions lead to lasting happiness, and which interactions lead to emotional distance and divorce.

In the bestselling book *Blink* (Little Brown, 2005), journalist Malcolm Gladwell refers to our process as "thin slicing." Simply put, this means we're able to quickly determine a great deal of information about a couple from analyzing a very thin slice of data collected in one short lab session. The reason our swift analysis works is because each thin slice of data is actually grounded in a tremendous amount of "thick slicing"—i.e., huge volumes of data that we've been collecting and validating on thousands of other couples for more than thirty years.

To help everyday couples use these discoveries to improve their own marriages, we established the Gottman Institute, which provides therapy and workshops for husbands and wives, as well as training for marriage therapists. Combining John's extensive research findings with Julie's thirty years of experience as a clinical psychologist, we've developed a body of advice that's based on two surprisingly simple truths:

1. Happily married couples behave like good friends.

In other words, their relationships are characterized by respect, affection, and empathy. They pay close attention to what's happening in each other's life and they feel emotionally connected. One of John's studies of couples discussing conflict demonstrated this well. It showed that spouses in happy, stable marriages made five positive remarks for every one negative remark when they were discussing conflict. In contrast, couples headed for divorce offered less than one (0.8) positive remark for every single negative remark.

2. Happily married couples handle their conflicts in gentle, positive ways.

They recognize that conflict is inevitable in any marriage, and that some problems never get solved, never go away. But these couples don't get gridlocked in their separate positions. Instead, they keep talking with each other about conflicts. They listen respectfully to their spouses' perspectives and they find compromises that work for both sides.

With this book, we give you an intimate view of ten couples who learned to work through serious problems that were threatening their marriages—problems like infidelity, overwork, adjustment to parenthood, unresolved anger and resentment, and a loss of interest in sex. You'll learn a bit about each couple's background and how they perceived the problems they brought to the Love Lab. You'll also read parts of the conversations that occurred when we asked husbands and wives to talk to each other about their problems.

For each couple, we present two dialogues, one that took place before we counseled them and one that happened after they heard our advice. In addition, you'll see a commentary alongside each dialogue titled "What We Noticed." This gives you a therapist's perspective on the interaction so that you might learn to detect some of the most common stumbling blocks that occur in relationships. You may notice, for example, places where a few words spoken in haste can take a conversation—and a marriage—down a dangerous path. You may learn to spot behaviors proven by John's research to damage relationships. These include a set of particularly poisonous patterns of interaction we call "the Four

Horsemen of the Apocalypse." Our studies have shown that, left unchecked, these behaviors can send couples into a downward spiral that ends in divorce. The Four Horsemen are

* CRITICISM. Often, criticism appears as a complaint or episode of blaming that's coupled with a global attack on your partner's personality or character. Criticism frequently begins with "you always" or "you never."

* DEFENSIVENESS. These are the counterattacks people use to defend their innocence or avoid taking responsibility for a problem. Defensiveness often takes the form of cross-complaining or whining.

* CONTEMPT. This is criticism bolstered by hostility or disgust. Think of somebody rolling their eyes while you're trying to tell them something important about yourself. Contempt often involves sarcasm, mocking, name-calling, or belligerence.

* STONEWALLING. This happens when listeners withdraw from the conversation, offering no physical or verbal cues that they're affected by what they hear. Interacting with somebody who does this is "like talking to a stone wall."

Our commentary also indicates the places where these couples make great strides—i.e., where they say or do something that strengthens the relationship by making them feel closer, encouraging compromise, or healing old wounds. Examples of such positive behaviors include

* SOFTENED START-UP. This is the ability to start talking about a complaint or a problem gently, without criticizing or insulting your partner. When one spouse does this, the other is more willing to listen, making compromise possible.

* TURNING TOWARD YOUR PARTNER. Close relationships consist of a series of "emotional bids"—that is, your partner

reaches out for emotional connection with a comment, a question, a smile, or a hug. You can choose to

1. *turn away, ignoring the bid*
2. *turn against, reacting with anger or hostility*
3. *turn toward, showing you're open, listening, and engaged*

Our research shows that habitually turning away or turning against your partner's bids harms your marriage. But consistently turning toward your partner strengthens emotional bonds, friendship, and romance.

* REPAIRING THE CONVERSATION. This is an effort to de-escalate negative feelings during a difficult encounter. A repair can be an apology, a smile, or bit of humor that breaks the tension and helps you both feel more relaxed.

* ACCEPTING INFLUENCE. Partners who are open to persuasion from each other generally have stronger, happier marriages. Being stubborn or domineering has just the opposite effect. Our studies show that a husband's willingness to accept influence from his wife can be particularly helpful to forming a strong, happy marriage.

Such concepts may seem familiar to people who have read John's previous books or attended our workshops. The difference with this book is that it invites you right into the Love Lab. Reading it, you spend time with ten couples who agreed to let us share their stories so that the work we did together might also help others. (For privacy, we've used fictional names and changed some identifying characteristics, but the situations and the conversations you'll read are real.)

Unlike books that simply *tell* you how to change your marriage, this book actually *shows* you how that transformation happens—how real couples talking about truly difficult problems can change the dynamics of their conversations; how they can stop having the same painful, destructive interactions over and over again and move on to a more peaceful coexistence. You see how they take the tools we suggest and use them to build back that sense of affection and romance that attracted them to each other in the first place.

In addition, each chapter provides quizzes you can take to see if you and your partner face the same problems these couples are overcoming. And we offer exercises you can do to make the same kind of progress these couples do.

As you read about these couples' progress, you may notice that many of the changes they make are small, simple adjustments—not big, complicated ones. A husband may, for example, learn to ask his wife more questions about how she's feeling. Or a wife may learn to express more appreciation for all the work her husband's been doing. We might advise a couple to stop and take a break to calm down when they're in the middle of a heated discussion. Or we might give them strategies for going to a deeper level in their conversations, sharing their hopes and dreams.

While the changes we suggest may not always seem like a big deal, our research shows that small, positive behaviors, frequently repeated, can make a *big* difference in the long-term success of a marriage. You could compare this work to piloting a plane cross-country. A turn of a few degrees over Ohio may seem like a small adjustment—merely fine-tuning. But in the long run it determines whether you end up in San Francisco or Los Angeles. So it is with a long-term relationship. When both partners commit to making small but consistently positive shifts in their interactions, they can take their marriage to a much happier place. And it's easier to assimilate small changes, rather than big ones.

Whether you're currently in a distressed relationship or you simply want to make a strong, happy relationship even better, we believe this book can help. It will show you what it's like to work with an effective therapist to improve your marriage. And it will also give you insights and tools you can use to make progress with or without counseling.

We hope that as you read this book, you find it comforting that you're not alone in your desire to make marriage better; that the challenges you and your partner may face are *not* insurmountable. And don't be surprised if you recognize yourselves in the situations and dialogues that follow. Our work has shown us that every couple is unique, but we also see many, many similarities. And that's a great sign that we can all learn from one another.

Best wishes,
John and Julie Gottman

CHAPTER 1

"All You Ever Do Is Work"

Sam remembers that falling in love with Katie was easy. The newest member of his coed softball team, she was "attractive, intelligent, and fun."

Holding on to her was harder. Soon after their first date, Katie left for a two-year Peace Corps job in Paraguay. Sam kept the courtship alive by sending Katie passionate letters. He would join her in South America at the end of her stint, he promised, and they would spend several weeks touring exotic destinations together.

Katie consented. "He was nice, fun, and witty," she recalls. And traveling with a man would feel safer than traveling alone. "But I thought he was crazy for writing those letters. We didn't even know each other!"

Ten years of marriage and three kids have certainly changed that. In Love Lab interviews and questionnaires, Katie and Sam reveal that they understand each other quite well. They also see eye to eye when it comes to tricky issues around parenting and finances.

But the Minneapolis couple has some serious challenges, too. During our initial meeting, Katie complains that Sam works far too much. She says he puts in so many hours at his job as a scientist for a small

What's the Problem?

- Katie's complaints about Sam's work slip into criticism.
- Sam defends himself and launches a counterattack.
- Katie gets defensive, angry, and more critical.
- Cycle of criticize/defend/countercriticize continues.
- Sam withdraws.
- Katie feels alone and frustrated.

What's the Solution?

- Learn to complain without criticizing.
- Hear the longing in each other's complaints.
- Express appreciation for each other.

biotech firm that he often has no energy left for the family. "Sam can be a great dad," Katie says. But when he takes time off, he's often too preoccupied and tired to play with their kids, aged six years, four years, and eighteen months, she explains.

Katie works part-time as a biochemist herself, so she understands how compelling Sam's work can be. But she feels strongly that, for the sake of their marriage, Sam needs to strike a better balance between work and family.

Katie also wants more of Sam's attention herself. After they put the kids to bed, he often disappears into his basement office until the wee hours, she complains. She'd like him to come to bed with her and cuddle. Whatever happened to the guy who wrote those passionate love letters, she wonders. Why can't he understand that she'd still like to see his romantic side?

Meanwhile, Sam's got his own complaints. Katie doesn't seem to appreciate how hard he works for the family's benefit. He feels that all he gets from her are criticism and demands. She should understand that when he's grappling with a difficult problem at work, it's hard for him to just "turn his brain off" and focus on the family, he explains. If he's going to relax, he needs more "down time," more solitude. Katie's requests for attention just make him want to withdraw.

Such complaints are common among couples who juggle demanding jobs with raising children. There really are just twenty-four hours in each day, and partners are bound to disagree over the way each person spends time. Since such conflicts aren't likely to disappear, the couple's challenge is to learn to live with their differences without harming the relationship. By the time Katie and Sam visited the Love Lab, however, they were beginning to lose confidence in their ability to get along.

"When we try to talk about our problems, we get angry so quickly," says Katie. "And then Sam can't stand to be in the same room with me, so he leaves. It just makes me crazy."

"Usually some trivial issue causes a disagreement," adds Sam. "And then, because we can't communicate, it just flares."

To learn more about the way they handle conflict, we ask Sam and Katie to talk to each other about a disagreement for ten minutes. We videotape the conversation. We also have them wear electrodes on their hands and abdomens so we can measure any physiological signs of stress, such as increases in heart rate, while they're talking. After the conversation, we analyze the tape and physiological data for information about the way their interactions are affecting their relationship.

On the next page, you'll see some excerpts from that conversation. In the left-hand column, you can read what Sam and Katie say. We recommend that you read that first. Then you can go back and look at the notes on the right-hand side for some of our observations about the conversation. Like "color commentary" from a sports announcer, these notes on the right may give you a little more insight into the successes and errors of this, a marital team. Comments preceded by a plus (+) sign indicate that the statement is having a generally favorable effect on the interaction. Comments preceded by a minus (−) sign indicate a generally negative effect. As you read, see if you can detect patterns in their interaction. Pay attention especially to moments when Katie or Sam goes from complaining to criticism, and what effect that has on the other person. Then read our analysis at the end of the dialogue and the advice we give.

11

What They Say	What We Notice
Katie: You were working so much of the time last summer. It felt like even when you were physically present, you weren't emotionally present. And I am really scared of that happening again.	+ Starts gently. + Complains without blaming him. + Talks clearly about her feelings.
Sam: The work is so important to me. It defines who I am.	− Doesn't respond to her expression of feelings. − Slightly defensive. + States his need.
Katie: I know. And when it heats up again, I don't want the same thing to happen. We were angry at each other all the time.	− Quickly dismisses his heartfelt statement. + Uses "we"; shows she shares responsibility for the problem.
Sam: Yeah. I remember that.	+ Validates her statement.
Katie: I don't want to go back there. So I would really like to figure out a way for you to still be able to be part of the family even when your work is busy and stressful. Then you could get the appreciation that you need from me, which you didn't get this last summer because I was so angry at you. I was so lonely because you were so not there.	+ Takes responsibility for part of the problem. + Tries to repair problems. + Expresses her feelings. − Slightly critical at the end.

What They Say	*What We Notice*
Sam: Yeah, when I'm busy with work, it's just in my head all the time.	+ Clarifies.
Katie: And so the family is just supposed to take a backseat.	− Criticizes with sarcasm.
Sam: No.	− Slightly defensive (short response).
Katie: We're just supposed to live without you for months.	− Criticizes.
Sam: No.	− Defensive.
Katie: Because you were physically there, but you were not emotionally present for a long time.	− Criticizes.
Sam: I'm not disagreeing. But I don't feel like you respect my work. You don't value that I'm working really hard. It's like everybody wants a piece of me. You just want another piece of me.	− Defensive. + Expresses his feelings. − Complaint turns to criticism.
Katie: That's reasonable for me to want a piece of you. You're my husband! You're supposed to be my best friend, my confidant, my support.	− Defensive. − Criticizes him again. − Doesn't respond to his complaint.

continued

What They Say	What We Notice
Sam: You want my support, and I wasn't getting any support from you. All I got was more demands.	– Defensive. – Countercriticizes.

After a while, the conversation moves into Katie's complaint about bedtime.

What They Say	What We Notice
Katie: I would love to go to bed together at the same time.	+ Starts gently. + Avoids blaming.
Sam: And I often get in bed and talk to you for a little bit and then I want to go off and watch the TV or . . .	– Slightly defensive. + States his need (to watch TV).
Katie: That's not really getting in bed with me. When you lie on top of the covers and I'm under the covers. I mean, I don't know if the physical stuff means anything to you, but it does to me.	– Interrupts. – Ignores his stated desire. + Clarifies her need.
Sam: Even though the physical stuff—is just touching?	+ Asks a question to clarify her need.
Katie: Yeah.	+ Validates.
Sam: It means something to me.	+ Validates, clarifies his feelings.

What They Say	What We Notice
Katie: I want to put my head on your bare shoulder.	+ Further clarifies her need.
Sam: I think you want me to be there to go to sleep. Which I would like to do, but I want to also have some downtime by myself.	+ Restates her needs. + States his own need of wanting time alone.
Katie: And you do get downtime by yourself. I mean, without staying up till three in the morning.	− Slightly defensive.
Sam: Yeah. Some evenings I do, but that's not the way it usually is. Usually, by the time the kids are in bed, you want to talk, and you want to talk all evening.	− Defensive. − Criticizes her needs.
Katie: Sam, that's not true. I can't remember an evening where we sat and talked all evening.	− Defensive.
Sam: That's what you would like.	− Criticizes.
Katie: But I can't remember one where we have actually done it. What I'd really like is just to feel connected to you.	− Defensive. + Expresses her need.
Sam: Yeah.	+ Validates.

continued

15

What They Say	*What We Notice*
Katie: Part of it is that I would really love to cuddle and we would probably have a better love life. And part of it is that when you stay up so late at night, you're exhausted.	+ Expresses her needs.
Sam: Yeah. OK. So you want more of me. You want me to be—	+ Restates her needs.
Katie: Emotionally there. You can be so much fun with the kids. You can actually be this wonderful father. And I love seeing you that way. And when you're exhausted, you're short with the kids. You have no patience. You yell at them.	− Interrupts him. + Expresses appreciation. + Expresses her needs. − Criticizes him.
Sam: The thing is, I would like to change all of that stuff. But I feel compelled to stay up late. I feel compelled to—	+ Expresses his feelings.
Katie: But those are all choices you make. You're the only one that can control your life.	− Interrupts him. − Criticizes.
Sam: I know. But when you're being antagonistic instead of being supportive of me changing, it isn't helping.	− Defensiveness. − Counterattack. − Blaming.

Our Analysis: A Cycle of Criticize/ Defend/Countercriticize

What patterns do you notice in Sam and Katie's interactions? Here's what we see:

On the positive side, Katie does a great job at the beginning of the conversation by bringing up problems in a gentle, nonconfrontational way—something we call "softened start-up." This is essential for couples who want to connect emotionally and build understanding. She also states her needs without blaming Sam. She simply describes how his behavior (working long hours; staying up late) affects her and how she feels about it.

To his credit, Sam initially responds to Katie's complaints by taking some responsibility for their problems. But he never really acknowledges Katie's feelings of loneliness and frustration. Then, after a few exchanges, the real trouble begins: Katie's complaints turn to criticism. In other words, she goes from simply revealing *her* feelings to making negative statements about *his* faults. Instead of describing specific problems, she paints the dispute as long lasting and global. ("We're just supposed to live without you *for months.*" ". . . you were not emotionally present *for a long time.*") We also notice a bit of hurtful sarcasm sneaking into her tone with statements like "The family is supposed to take a backseat."

Sam's response is typical for a partner under attack. He doesn't empathize or express understanding. He simply defends himself and eventually starts launching a counteroffensive. ("You want my support, and I wasn't getting any support from you.") This, in turn, causes Katie to become defensive, setting up an all-too-common cycle of criticize/ defend/countercriticize—a pattern that can cause arguments to escalate out of control.

Fortunately, such escalation doesn't happen for Katie and Sam in this conversation. That's because Katie does a masterful job of pulling the plug after just a few exchanges; she agrees with Sam that she has indeed been demanding. ("Right," she responds, "you're absolutely right.") This temporary cease-fire allows Sam to tell Katie more about his needs, and Katie—thank goodness—listens. It doesn't take long, however, for the criticism and defensiveness to creep back into their exchange. And by the end of the conversation, Katie's frustration is palpable and Sam is withdrawing. If this conversation occurred in their bedroom instead of our lab, Sam probably would be headed for the basement and some downtime, leaving Katie to seethe.

Our Advice

We suggest that Katie and Sam try a second conversation about their differences. Only this time we give them three specific pieces of advice:

1. COMPLAIN WITHOUT CRITICIZING

Katie and Sam both have valid complaints. Katie feels she needs more help with parenting and more romantic attention from Sam. Sam feels he needs more respect from Katie for all the hard work and the financial support he's providing. So the most important change we recommend for Katie and Sam is to learn to express those needs without criticizing each other's character or personality. Constant criticism can be very harmful to a relationship. Unchecked, it can even put marriages on a downhill course that ends in divorce. But if Katie and Sam can learn to state their needs in a more healthy way (see "Healthy Complaining Versus Harmful Complaining" on page 25), they can break the cycle of criticize/defend/countercriticize that's causing prolonged and contentious arguments.

Avoiding criticism is particularly important if you're married to somebody who is highly sensitive to others' disapproval. Through our interviews, we learn this may be true for Sam, who was raised in a military family—a culture that some psychologists believe makes kids quite vulnerable to criticism. (See "The 'Oversensitive' Partner," page 29.) Both Sam and Katie report that Sam seems to take even the most minor negative statements to heart, as though he were bracing himself for the blow that hasn't happened yet, but seems sure to come.

18

To help Sam cope with this sensitivity, we advise Katie to ask Sam questions about his behaviors. By showing genuine interest in his desire to work so much, for example, she may help him to open up to her so they can discuss the issue more deeply. This, in turn, may eventually lead to better understanding and a solution to their conflict.

2. LOOK FOR THE LONGING IN EACH OTHER'S COMPLAINTS

It's clear to us that Sam wants more understanding and appreciation from Katie. And although Katie doesn't always express it, it's also clear to us that she appreciates Sam very much. That's why she wants to spend more time with him. She wants to enjoy his sense of humor, she wants to share the fun of raising their kids together, and she wants to share more intimacy in bed.

The trouble is, Sam isn't hearing that longing. All he's hearing is Katie's irritability and discontent. When Katie says, "I love to feel your skin and cuddle with you," all Sam hears is, "Once again, she thinks I'm inadequate."

Our advice for Sam is to listen more closely to the longing in Katie's complaints. And if he's not sure what she's longing for when she complains, ask questions. "What does spending time together in bed at the end of the day mean to you?" he might ask. "Tell me why this is important."

Katie might ask Sam more questions about his complaints as well—questions like "What would it mean for you to feel that I respect and support your work? Why is that important to you? What would it look like?"

3. EXPRESS AND ACCEPT APPRECIATION

Both Katie and Sam say they feel unappreciated in their marriage, which is too bad, since both of them are working harder than ever, and they're doing it for the sake of their shared interest—their family. This seeming lack of appreciation is common for many young, busy couples—especially during periods of high stress at work, or unusually tough family demands. Operating in survival mode, each partner feels exhausted and may not have the extra energy it takes to say, "Thanks for doing the taxes," or "I really appreciated that you got up at two a.m. to feed the baby." But when partners don't hear expressions of appreciation, they feel taken for granted and their feelings of stress just get worse.

This seems to be true for Katie and Sam when he's working long hours and she's caring for the kids on her own. So we suggest that they make a more conscious effort to notice good deeds the other does. We tell them to try to "catch each other in the act of getting it right." Then speak up. Tell each other that you see and appreciate the good things each is bringing to the family.

While we notice that Katie expresses quite a bit of appreciation for Sam, he doesn't necessarily hear and internalize the appreciation that she offers. We suspect that's because Katie's praise is often coupled with criticism. (Remember how she starts to tell him he's a "wonderful father" only to conclude, "You have no patience. You yell at them.") This contrast is a testament to the terrible negative power of criticism, which may be undoing all of Katie's best intentions to build Sam up.

Another problem is that Sam has a hard time accepting Katie's appreciation. "I don't understand her love for me sometimes," he tells us. "I don't know where it comes from." So here's another piece of advice for Sam: Give yourself the benefit of the doubt. Even if Katie's love seems irrational to you at times, open yourself up to it. When she expresses appreciation, make a mental note and repeat that conversation in your mind. Over time, you may learn to accept this fact: You are truly worthy, and you are truly loved.

Here are some excerpts from a second conversation, where Sam and Katie try out our advice:

What They Say	What We Notice
Katie: I want to hear more about why your work is so important to you.	+ Opens with a supportive question.
Sam: First, I want to tell you something that you probably don't know. I like that you want to cuddle with me. I appreciate that you want that.	+ Expresses appreciation.
Katie: I'm glad you like it, because I like it, too.	+ Expresses gratitude, appreciation.
Sam: Now, about my work, I get a sense of self-worth from doing the complex and technical stuff.	+ Responsive, expressing his feelings.
Katie: So is that why your mind doesn't let go of it?	+ Open-ended, exploratory question.
Sam: When I'm thinking about something, it's just what my mind does. It's not a conscious thing. It's just that my mind takes me there.	+ Responsive, clarifying.
Katie: Do you get the self-worth from your work even when your work is not as time-consuming and demanding?	+ Exploratory question.

continued

What They Say	What We Notice
Sam: Yeah, but it doesn't have to do with recognition from other people. It has to do with me feeling like I've done a good job for myself. That's where my self-esteem comes from. It's important to me that I've come up with an elegant solution or whatever.	+ Responsive, expressing his feelings.
Katie: That must feel good.	+ Communicates empathy and approval.
Sam: Yeah, it does feel good. I appreciate you asking me about it. It feels really nice.	+ Expresses appreciation and feelings.
Eventually, the topic shifts to bedtime.	
Sam: I would like to devote time to you each evening. What holds me back is I feel like it's an obligation instead of something I'm doing because I want to do it. I feel like it's being demanded of me as opposed to something I'm giving freely.	+ Expresses willingness to meet her need. + Honestly expresses that he feels obligated by her demand. + Not blaming.
Katie: I really do appreciate the fact that you want to spend some time with me in the evening. But I think even if I said, "Can I have a half hour of your time?" you would still hear criticism. Even if I don't say, "We haven't done it all week," you might still hear, "God, I haven't done that. She doesn't think I do that enough."	+ Expresses appreciation. + Honestly expresses fear that he won't be able to hear her needs without thinking she's criticizing him.

What They Say	What We Notice
Sam: That's true. You're right. I am very likely to hear that. But over time, if we practice, I think we probably can do better.	+ Accepts responsibility and expresses hope.
Katie: Is there something else I should say that would help?	+ Good exploratory question.
Sam: If you would tell me what you want without focusing on what my behavior has been in the past—that would go a long way. Even if you did that, I might hear my own subtext of criticism for a while. But I could practice trying to listen more to your words. Maybe you could joke about it. That might click in my mind, "She really is trying to keep it positive."	+ States need for her to avoid focusing on the past. + Accepts responsibility. + Expresses willingness to find solution.
Katie: So what if I just make it more light—add some joke to make it more positive?	+ Good summarizing, clarifying.
Sam: Yeah, that would go a long way, I think.	+ Validating.

By the end of the conversation, Sam and Katie seem relieved. Katie's questions show that she is genuinely interested in Sam's experience. This, in turn, encourages him to open up to her. The validating remarks and statements of appreciation they share keep the conversation on a positive track so that they can talk peacefully and productively about their problems. Noticeably absent are statements of criticism and defensiveness.

For the first time, Katie can see how the criticism in her complaints affects Sam and their relationship. And she understands that even when she's not being particularly critical, Sam may still hear her words in that way.

Sam explains that he now realizes how much he wants to respond to Katie's longing. "When I don't feel criticized, I want to give you what you want, what you need," he tells her.

One Year Later

We check back with Sam and Katie a year later, and here's what we find: Sam is still working long hours and Katie still wishes he wouldn't. Are we surprised? Not at all. Sam and Katie's differences over Sam's work are a classic example of what we call a "perpetual issue"—i.e., a disagreement that will never go away. (For more about this, see the section titled "Don't Get Gridlocked over Perpetual Issues" in chapter 10.)

Every long-term relationship has its share of perpetual issues. In fact, our research shows that some 69 percent of all marital conflicts can be categorized as never ending. What can change, however, is a couple's willingness to accept their differences and to improve their skills at solving problems that result.

That's one way Sam and Katie have changed over the past year. Katie says she has learned to accept Sam's passion for his work and his long hours as part of who he is. "So now I make a conscious effort not to give him a hard time about it, because that's what he wants to do," she says.

Sam, in turn, appreciates the changes in Katie. "The criticism is just not there anymore and that makes a huge difference to me," he reports.

Sam is also seeing Katie's needs from a new perspective. "Before, when she would ask me not to work, I felt like she was attacking me. Now I'm more likely to take a breath and remember that she just wants to be with me, that's all. She's just asking for some of my time." As a result, he says he feels less defensive and more willing to do what she's asking.

HEALTHY COMPLAINING VERSUS HARMFUL COMPLAINING

It's a myth that happily married people don't complain about each other's behavior. In fact, it would be ludicrous to expect two human beings to live together without complaints. We all have our own idiosyncratic needs, desires, rhythms, and habits. And these needs are bound to collide, producing strong emotions.

Constantly stifling your complaints is not a good idea. Doing so can cause you to hold on to angry, resentful feelings toward your partner. You may develop a state of mind we call "negative sentiment override," where your bad thoughts about your partner and relationship overwhelm and override any positive thoughts about them. You may start to stockpile your grievances, keeping track of each offense your partner commits. In the meantime, your bad feelings fester and grow, resulting in one of two outcomes: You either distance yourself emotionally to avoid the pain or you lash out. Meanwhile, your offending partner, who rarely hears a negative word from you, is in the dark. There's little chance for your partner to improve his or her ability to meet your needs because your partner doesn't know what's wrong— that is, until you hit your limit and explode with a barrage of grievances you've been saving up.

There is an alternative to either stifling or exploding, however. Partners can learn to express their needs (i.e., complain) in ways that are respectful, clear, specific, and immediate. There are many benefits to this approach. For example, your partner is more likely to hear your complaint and respond to it if you express it in this way, and complaining in a healthy way actually helps to solve problems, build intimacy, and strengthen the relationship.

Here are examples:

Healthy Complaining	Harmful Complaining
Share responsibility for the problem: "We haven't been able to afford a vacation in two years. Maybe we should work out a better budget."	**Blame the problem on the other person:** "It's all your fault that we can't afford a vacation. You waste our money on stupid things."
Describe the problem in terms of your perception, opinion, or style: "I'm just more conservative about money and I think you spent too much for that pair of shoes."	**Describe the problem as a matter of absolute truth:** "Anybody can see that's too much money to spend on a pair of shoes."
Focus on a specific problem, tackling one at a time: "You set your glass on the coffee table last night and now there's a ring."	**Stockpile complaints:** "You haven't done the laundry in two weeks, the lawn needs mowing, and you never cleaned the garage like you said you would."
	Make broad, sweeping statements: "You never take me anywhere."

Healthy Complaining	Harmful Complaining
Focus on the present:	**Dig up past grievances:**
"You said you would help Sean with his homework, but you're still watching TV."	"You didn't cook one meal the whole time I was putting you through law school."
Focus on partner's actions and how those actions make you feel:	**Criticize your partner's personality or character:**
"I thought we were going to have a romantic evening together, and you invited your mother. I feel so hurt and disappointed."	"I thought we were going to have a romantic evening together, and you invited your mother. How can you be such a clueless, insensitive dolt?"
Pick a time to complain about the problem when partner can listen and respond.	**Complain at times when partner is distracted by pressing matters such as a deadline or caring for small children.**
Tell partner about your needs and desires:	**Don't complain. Expect your partner to mind-read, to guess your needs and desires.**
"I feel so tired that I need to just cuddle with you right now. Maybe tomorrow we can make love."	She moves away from his touch with no explanation.
	continued

Healthy Ways to Respond to a Complaint	Harmful Ways to Respond to a Complaint
Rephrase the complaint so the complainer knows you understand: "So you're upset because I'm an hour late."	**Ignore the complaint altogether.**
Ask questions for a better understanding: "Do you want me to call you if I'm going to be late?" "You say you want more of my attention. Do you feel like we don't talk enough?"	**Belittle or criticize your partner for complaining:** "I can't believe you're upset because I'm an hour late. You're such a control freak." "You want more of my attention? You want me to sit here and stare at you all day?"
Acknowledge the feelings behind your partner's complaint: "I forgot it was Valentine's Day. You must feel hurt and angry."	**Defend yourself:** "I forgot it was Valentine's Day because I was so focused on my training. I've got to make a living, you know!"
	Use sarcasm or criticism: "What do you want me to do—cancel my training because it's Valentine's Day?" "If you had a real job, you wouldn't have time to obsess about Valentine's Day."
Take responsibility for the problem: "You're right. I should have been nicer to your mom."	**Deny responsibility for the problem:** "It's not my fault that your mom is so touchy."

THE "OVERSENSITIVE" PARTNER

Some people seem to react very strongly to complaints and criticism, making it hard for their partners to talk about needs that aren't being met. Such high sensitivity is often the result of patterns set in childhood. People who grow up in families with problems such as substance abuse or emotional, physical, or sexual abuse, for example, may be more sensitive to criticism than others. That's because small children are so naturally egocentric that they falsely believe their actions can cause or prevent family problems and instability. *("If I'm just good enough, Mom won't yell at me." "Dad would still be here if I hadn't talked back to him.")* Kids from military families, where a parent sometimes has to leave unexpectedly, may experience the same type of problems. *("If I can just make Dad happy, maybe he won't ship out again.")* What's the result when kids constantly feel responsible for unfortunate circumstances beyond their control? They grow up feeling compelled to defend themselves, to say constantly, "It's not my fault." If they hear a complaint, they automatically brace themselves. They prepare to fight back whether they're under attack or not.

This can be a real struggle in a close partnership or marriage. What starts out as a simple conversation about one person's needs can easily turn into a full-fledged battle. An example:

"We need to balance the checkbook."

"I'm not the one writing all those checks!"

"I thought you wrote one to the hair salon just yesterday."

"So now I'm supposed to cut my own hair, is that it?"

What's the solution? If you're the highly sensitive partner:

* Listen carefully to the words your partner is saying when stating a need or making a request. Your partner may not be as critical as you first think.

* Be aware of times that you automatically react by defending yourself. Can you think of a different reaction instead?

* See what happens when you take a deep breath and agree. *("OK. Let's balance the checkbook tonight.")*

* Try asking your partner to tell you more about the need or complaint. *("Why do you like to balance the checkbook every two weeks?")*

If your partner is highly sensitive:

* Take extra care to avoid criticism when stating your needs. (See section called "Healthy Complaining Versus Harmful Complaining" on page 25.)

* If your partner responds defensively, avoid responding the same way.

* Respond to defensiveness by clarifying your statement of need. *("I'd just like to balance the checkbook to make sure that we don't get overdrawn.")*

When One Partner Works Too Much

Katie's complaint that Sam works too much is a common one. Many people believe their relationships would improve if their partners would stop working long hours and start putting more energy into the marriage. And in many cases, the complaining partner is right. Strong marriages require two partners who are willing to give their time and attention to each other.

If you're the overworking spouse, you may be reacting to pressures in the workplace—a demanding boss, for instance, or your employer's threat to lay off less productive workers. Maybe you're under financial stress; you feel that you've got to work long hours simply to make ends meet.

Or perhaps your own attitude toward your work makes you feel compelled to work long hours. Like Sam, you may feel that your profession is your identity, that your job is "who I am." If this is true for you, you probably feel most comfortable when you're in the workplace, doing your job, and doing it well. There's nothing wrong with this, of course. In fact, for many people, it's ideal. But if you find that you're consistently putting in so many hours that your spouse feels emotionally disconnected from you, your attitude toward work may be putting your marriage at risk.

What can couples do to change this dynamic? You may find it helpful to have a conversation like the one that Sam and Katie had—one that explores two sets of questions.

1. To the spouse who is overworking, questions include:

- *What does your work mean to you?*

- *What pleasure or satisfaction does work bring to you?*

- *What need does working fulfill in your life?*

- *Does your work relate to some personal legacy you'd like to contribute to the world?*

2. To the spouse who is complaining about overwork, questions include:

- *What does your spouse's absence mean to you?*

- *What positive things do you miss about your partner when he or she is gone so much?*

- *What are you longing for in terms of emotional, physical, intellectual, or spiritual connection with your partner?*

continued

As you explore these questions, remember to avoid criticizing your partner's position, or defending your own. Listen carefully and express appreciation for the contribution each person brings to the marriage.

If you're the spouse who is complaining about your partner's long hours, try to express your longing in a positive way.

If you're the spouse who is working long hours, listen carefully to your partner's complaint, zeroing in on the yearning behind it. As you talk, don't focus on the behaviors that your spouse would like to eliminate—habits like evening meetings, cell-phone calls, or work-related e-mail during a family vacation. Instead, visualize the experiences your spouse might like you to have as a result of working less—perhaps a romantic vacation, relaxing evenings at home, or better relationships with the kids.

The key is to help the overworking spouse to understand this: *Your life is valuable far beyond what you contribute as a worker and a wage earner. You are also loved, appreciated, and needed as a friend, lover, confidant, co-parent, traveling companion, and so on.*

Couples who can share this sense of appreciation toward each other feel a strong sense of emotional connection. This, in turn, makes it easier to discuss conflicts related to work. Some may see their conflict in a new light and choose to make big life changes. Others may decide to maintain the status quo as Katie and Sam did, but they do so with a better acceptance of each other's feelings about the issue of work. When couples experience less criticism and more appreciation, a happier marriage becomes possible—*despite* the ongoing difference of opinion about how much work is too much.

The exercise at the end of this chapter, called "What's Your Mission? What's Your Legacy?" may also help. It's designed to assist couples in clarifying and communicating their priorities in life, including the value work holds for individual partners.

Quiz: Is There Too Much Criticism in Your Relationship?

The following quiz can help you see how well you and your partner state your needs (i.e., complain) without resorting to harmful criticism. Take the quiz twice. The first time, answer the questions for yourself. The second time, answer the questions the way you believe your partner would answer them.

PARTNER A		PARTNER B
T/F		T/F
____	1. I often feel attacked or criticized when we talk about our disagreements.	____
____	2. I often have to defend myself because the things my partner says about me are so unfair.	____
____	3. When I complain, I think it's important to present many examples of what my partner does wrong.	____
____	4. When my partner complains, I often just want to leave the scene.	____
____	5. I think it's important to point out when problems are not my fault.	____
____	6. I often feel insulted when my partner complains.	____
____	7. I think my partner should know what I need without my having to say it.	____
____	8. I often feel as though my personality is being assaulted.	____
____	9. When I complain, I think it's important to show my partner the moral basis for my position.	____
____	10. I often think my partner is selfish and self-centered.	____
____	11. I am not guilty of many things my partner accuses me of.	____
____	12. Small issues often escalate out of proportion.	____

continued

PARTNER A		PARTNER B
T/F		T/F

PARTNER A T/F		PARTNER B T/F
____	13. My partner's feelings get hurt too easily.	____
____	14. I often feel disgusted by some of my partner's attitudes.	____
____	15. My partner uses phrases such as "you always" or "you never" when complaining.	____
____	16. I think it's helpful to point out ways my partner can improve his or her personality.	____
____	17. When I complain to my partner, I think it's helpful to mention examples of other people who do things the way I'd like them to be done.	____
____	18. I often think to myself, "Who needs all this conflict?"	____
____	19. If I have to ask my partner for a compliment or a favor, then it really doesn't count.	____
____	20. I often feel disrespected by my partner.	____

SCORING: If you have more than four "true" answers either time you take the test, you may have a problem with too much criticism in your relationship. Use the tips in the section titled "Healthy Complaining Versus Harmful Complaining" to reduce the criticism.

Exercise: Listen for the Longing Behind Your Partner's Complaints

Below is a list of common marital complaints. Often partners complain because they long for something good or healing to happen in their relationship. Here are some examples of such complaints, followed by the positive desire the complainer has for the relationship:

Complaint: Why do you always let the garbage pile up like this?

Longing: I wish that we could feel more like teammates taking care of our house.

34

Complaint: You never call me during the day.

Longing: I wish we could feel close to each other, even when we're apart.

Complaint: I'm tired of making dinner every night.

Longing: I'd like to go out to dinner with you, as we did when we were dating.

Now, see if you can imagine the positive desire behind the following complaints. Take turns reading a complaint out loud and have your partner supply the longing behind the complaint.

Complaint: It seems like so long since we've had any fun.

Longing: _____

Complaint: We haven't had sex in weeks. What's wrong with you?

Longing: _____

Complaint: I never seem to get personal presents for my birthday.

Longing: _____

Complaint: I'm just too tired to go grocery shopping.

Longing: _____

Complaint: If you keep spending like this, we'll go bankrupt.

Longing: _____

Complaint: I hate it when your mother drops by without calling first.

Longing: _____

Now list some complaints you commonly hear from your partner. Then each of you write a statement about the longing that's behind that complaint.

Complaint: _____

Longing: _____

Complaint: _____

Longing: _____

Complaint: _____

Longing: _____

Complaint: _____

Longing: _____

Complaint: _____

Longing: _____

Complaint: _____

Longing: _____

Exercise: What's Your Mission? What's Your Legacy?

This exercise comes from Julie's experience counseling patients with terminal illness. She saw that most people, in the face of their own deaths, have little trouble setting priorities. They know what matters most.

Through our workshops, we've learned that visualizing the end of your own life may have similar benefits. You come to understand your own values better. And that helps you make choices about how to spend your time.

Read the following questions and jot down your ideas. Then discuss your ideas with your partner.

1. Imagine that a doctor has just told you that you have only six months to live. How would you choose to spend that time?

2. Imagine opening the newspaper the day after you die and seeing your own obituary. How would you like that obituary to read? How would you like people to think of your life, to remember you? What legacy would you like to leave behind?

3. Using ideas from steps one and two, write a mission statement for your life. What is your purpose? What is your life's meaning? What are the most important things you'd like to accomplish? What elements of your current life matter most to you? What matters least?

CHAPTER 2

"Will We Ever Get Over Your Affair?"

Maybe it was good fortune that David wanted most in a wife. That's certainly what attracted him to Candace when they first met at a church youth group when they were both sixteen years old.

"We were playing poker and Candace drew four aces and the joker," David recalls. "That really made an impression on me!"

Candace remembers the teenaged David as a soft-spoken, gentle boy. That notion never changed. "I've always thought of him as a good person, the sweetest man there is," she says. "He's really kind to me— my sweetheart and my best friend."

So imagine Candace's shock when, at forty, she learned that David was having an affair.

"It happened about two years ago," says David, a Pittsburgh-area real estate salesman. He'd been under a lot of pressure at the time. He had just invested—and lost—most of their retirement savings in a land deal that went sour.

"I hadn't fairly consulted with Candace, and I felt so bad about it," David said. Then he met a woman at his office who was willing to listen. "She really sympathized with me and I got involved with her. I never thought it was going to go that way, but unfortunately it did."

Candace found out about the affair in a phone call from the woman's husband. Feeling shattered, she confronted David. He didn't try to deny it. In fact, he confessed and ended the relationship with the other woman right away.

Then David and Candace went to work, doing everything they could think of to get their marriage back on track. Over the next two years they read every book they could find about healing their marriage. They went to marriage workshops. They even began co-teaching a class on marriage at their church. Still, it seemed a struggle to recover from the emotional upheaval the affair had caused. While David wrestled with feelings of guilt, Candace felt haunted by a recurring sense of betrayal.

Neither partner reports having had serious problems in their marriage prior to David's fling. Married at nineteen, the couple had two sons in their first four years together. David's sales job required lots of travel to other states, so he took his young family with him. Both he and Candace remember those early years as happy times, traveling by car, staying in motels, enjoying their time together. After

What's the Problem?

- *David and Candace avoid conflict; they don't share negative feelings.*

- *When Candace brings up a problem, David gets stressed.*

- *Instead of expressing understanding, David tries to reassure Candace that everything is OK.*

- *Candace feels unheard, frustrated.*

- *Candace gets stressed and shuts down.*

- *Emotional distance grows—a problem that contributed to David's affair.*

What's the Solution?

- *Say what you're feeling, what you need, even if it's difficult to handle.*

- *Listen and respond to each other's feelings and needs before you rush to reassure and before you try to solve problems.*

- *Recognize when you're stressed, and take steps to relax.*

- *Expect more, not less, from your marriage.*

the boys started school, Candace went to college and became a nurse while David concentrated on starting his real estate business.

Candace tells us they always tried to be "realistic" about marriage. "As you age, those big, passionate, 'teenage crush' feelings naturally go away—that's to be expected," she says. So, by their late thirties, she wasn't surprised that their romantic feelings for each other had waned. Having a strong friendship seemed good enough.

When she learned of David's affair, however, all of her ideas about a passionless marriage went up in smoke. "Now I could see that David still had the capacity for romance," Candace explains. "Passion doesn't have to go away just because we're growing older."

David swears he has totally recommitted to his marriage, and Candace seems to trust that that's true. Still, she finds herself wanting more from him than she ever needed before. In the aftermath of the affair, she needs to know on a much deeper level that she's number one.

David seems eager to reassure Candace, but he also admits that he has a hard time conveying his romantic feelings for her. Why? Both believe their hectic lifestyle is part of the problem. David claims they're always so busy trying to "get their ducks in a row" that they never take time for each other.

But we suspect there may be other obstacles to greater emotional intimacy. To find out, we ask Candace and David to talk to each other about a recent conflict. They start by discussing an incident that happened in the hotel room that morning, just before they came to the Love Lab.

What They Say	What We Notice
Candace: This morning I asked if you would massage my feet after you made your telephone calls. But it would have just thrilled my heart if you would have done the massage first. It would have made me feel like I was more important than the calls.	+ Good start; clearly expresses feelings. + States her need.
David: The problem is, you said, "You can do it after you call the office." And I already had my schedule planned out. But I wouldn't have minded doing that for you.	− Defensive. − Ignores her feelings of disappointment. − Responds with his own complaint. + Expresses willingness to respond to her request.
Candace: But that would have interrupted your plans.	− Doesn't acknowledge his willingness. − Slightly defensive. − Backs away from expressing her needs.
David: You said up front that it was OK for me to do these other things first. Then you seemed to get irritated. That's *my* source of irritation. You want me to read your mind. But I think we do pretty good over all, don't you?	− Slightly defensive. + States his complaint. − Tries to sweep the problem under the rug by praising the relationship. − Still doesn't acknowledge her feelings of disappointment. + Asks for reassurance, but is he asking for the suppression of emotion?

continued

41

What They Say	What We Notice
Candace: *(Nods yes.)*	− Stifles her feelings. − Doesn't respond to his attempt to deny their problems.
David: There are just certain things that we have problems with. Maybe we just need more communication.	− Minimizes her feelings. + Hesitantly refers to the problem again. − Tries prematurely to put a lid on the problem.
Candace *(through tears)*: I just feel . . . it makes me very sad when I am not your highest priority.	+ Tries again *(courageously)* to communicate her needs and feelings.
David: Do you feel like I do this a lot?	+ Asks a question without being defensive.
Candace *(wiping tears away)*: Most of the time you make me a high priority.	+/− Reassures him, but backs away from discussing her need.
David *(softly)*: Can you give me an example of when you think I don't?	+ Invites feedback without being defensive.
Candace: *(She sighs and says nothing.)*	− Still stifles her expression of sadness.

42

What They Say	What We Notice
David: I try to be flexible and I think I am. But if I don't understand, then maybe I'm not listening as well as I should.	— Somewhat defensive. +/— Takes responsibility, but in a general, vague way.
Candace: I don't know why I'm so tearful today. *(Long silence.)* I've lost my train of thought, I think.	— Stress causes her to "flood"; becoming upset interferes with her thinking and communication. — Doesn't ask for what she needs.

Our Analysis: Sidestepping Difficult Feelings Blocks Emotional Intimacy

On the surface, this couple seems to be handling their differences well. They show lots of concern and affection for each other; their tone is sweet and caring. Looking more closely, however, we can see the source of emotional distance: David and Candace are so intent on avoiding bad feelings that they're sidestepping issues that really need discussion. And David, especially, seems to be in such a rush to reassure Candace, he misses opportunities to demonstrate just how much he really cares.

Optimistic by nature, David and Candace have always placed a high value on getting along. And after David's affair threatened the security of their relationship, being accommodating and reassuring feels more important than ever. But when couples consistently avoid problems, they develop a habit of squelching their negative feelings. This creates emotional distance, which is a high price to pay for avoiding conflict. The price includes a sense of loneliness and a lack of romance. It's hard to be passionate toward your spouse when you don't feel close anymore.

43

Still, Candace has decided she will use this visit to the Love Lab as an opportunity to tell David what she needs. And in the dialogue above, she bravely states that she wants his physical affection, starting with a foot massage. Despite his initial defensiveness about the way Candace makes her request, David shows that he's open to her request. But he doesn't acknowledge how Candace is feeling in the moment. For example, he doesn't say, "I can see that you felt sad when I didn't stop and pay attention," or "I'm sorry that I missed your cue. That must have hurt your feelings."

Our guess is that David feels it's too risky to engage Candace in a conversation about her sadness. His heart rate, which we measured via electrodes attached to his chest and fingers, shows this may be true. At the beginning of the conversation it was already 100 beats per minute, which is higher than average—perhaps because he finds it stressful to be in the lab, poised to talk about problems. But it jumps even higher, up to 121 beats per minute, when Candace starts telling David about her disappointment. Such spikes are a sign of "diffuse physiological arousal," or "flooding." In other words, emotional stress has caused the many parts of his nervous system to become so overloaded that it's difficult for him to think straight and communicate, so he tries to put a lid on the conversation. But his attempts to reassure Candace and to repair the interaction don't do the trick because he's jumping to the conclusion. "I think we do pretty good, don't you?" he asks Candace. But nothing has happened yet to make *her* feel that things are pretty good.

What's the result? Candace doesn't seem to notice consciously that her needs have been dismissed. By all appearances, David is being his old sweet, reassuring self. So, despite her sadness, she nods, as if to say, "Yes, everything is just fine." But her heart is telling her something different, so she tries once more. ("It makes me very sad . . .") Only this time she doesn't wait for him to dismiss her feelings. She does it herself. Our heart monitor tells us her pulse is racing at 154 beats per minute, which causes her to clam up, full of tears. With her heart rate at this level, she's probably secreting the hormone adrenaline, as well. This

44

interferes with her ability to think clearly, and she withdraws. The interaction leaves both of them feeling hurt, frustrated, and confused because they can't see where they've gone wrong.

Our Advice

1. TELL YOUR PARTNER WHAT YOU NEED, EVEN IF IT FEELS DIFFICULT

It's clear to us that David and Candace need to do a better job of stating their needs to each other. Although Candace makes a strong bid for getting more attention from David, she backs down when David tells her everything is OK. She may be doing this because she wants so badly to get her marriage back on solid ground, but it's having just the opposite effect.

As Candace told us earlier, she and David gradually started to expect less romance in their relationship over time, believing that would make them happier in the long run. "Don't expect much and you won't be disappointed," they might have said. But now she sees that their strategy has backfired. And it's not surprising, considering what marriage researcher Donald Baucom has found. His studies show that couples who have high expectations for romance and passion in their relationships are more likely to have these qualities in their marriages than are those who have low expectations; and those with high expectations have happier marriages as a result.

Candace's habit of letting David off the hook does not make things better for this couple. Instead, it creates more distance. If Candace wants to grow closer to David, she's going to have to make sure she's heard by him, even if it creates the potential for more conflict. Avoiding the conflict will only make matters worse for them.

By the same token, David needs to let Candace know what's in his heart. Imagine what might have happened if David had been more open with Candace when he lost their retirement money. Imagine if he'd been able to tell her, "I feel terrible about this. I need your understanding. I need your forgiveness. I need your support." He badly wanted such sympathy at the time, but instead of turning to Candace, he turned to somebody outside the marriage for support. Because he was not able to express his deepest feelings to his wife, his marriage became prone to an affair long before the affair ever started. As marriage researcher Shirley Glass discovered, when partners avoid talking to each other about their deepest feelings, they put their marriage at risk for infidelity.

David and Candace say they understand this in hindsight. And they tell us they really want to change the way they interact. They want more emotional intimacy, they want to feel closer. But after twenty-three years of avoidance, how do they start sharing intense feelings with each other now?

One key is to believe that you can trust your partner to be receptive and nonjudgmental when you start to speak. You want to feel "safe" that your partner will listen carefully and with an open mind. She won't dismiss your feelings. He won't judge, criticize, or offer unsolicited advice. Once you achieve this sense of trust, you feel freer to stay with your feelings in the conversation and express them to your partner as they come up. Emotional flooding becomes less of a problem, which means you're less likely to withdraw.

To help Candace and David experience this, we suggest that they try another conversation in which they take turns at expressing what they need emotionally from the relationship and telling each other how they feel about the need. When it's one partner's turn, the other partner's job is to simply listen and ask questions that can lead to better understanding.

We give them some guidelines. We advise Candice, "Stick to your guns and don't withdraw. If David responds with reassurances that don't change—or even acknowledge—the way you're feeling, let him know that. You don't have to be unkind about it. You can simply hold your ground and say, 'I really want you to understand my feelings here.' "

2. "BROADCAST" YOUR FEELINGS AS THEY COME UP

To David we say, "When it's your turn, think about the emotions you're feeling and tell Candace about them as they come up. It's kind of like being a play-by-play radio broadcaster. Candace can't *see* what's going on inside your heart and your head. To help her follow the game, you've got to announce the plays." We explain that this may seem a little strange after twenty-three years of being the strong, steady, silent type in this relationship, but it gets easier with practice.

3. POSTPONE PROBLEM SOLVING UNTIL AFTER YOU FEEL CONNECTED

We encourage them both to stay with the strong emotions that may surface as they talk. Don't try to draw conclusions prematurely; doing so will be counterproductive.

And, finally, we advise them to avoid problem solving at this point. This conversation is not about solving problems; it's about opening a door to emotional intimacy and feeling closer to each other. Problem solving can come later.

David agrees to go first. Here's what happened.

What They Say	What We Notice
David: I need for you to open up and tell me what you're thinking. A lot of times, we just share facts. And sometimes when you start talking about feelings, you shut down. That really bothers me.	+ Starts gently. + Focuses on her feelings. − Still, he's not saying much about his own feelings, his own needs.
Candace: So you're saying you want me to tell you what I'm thinking and feeling? That's what you need from me?	+ Clarifies.

continued

What They Say	What We Notice
David: Yeah. Like with the foot massage, it would have helped if you had just said, "I need some time with you right now. I need to feel connected to you. And you could help me feel connected by putting this lotion on my feet."	+ Expresses what he wants from her without blaming, without defensiveness.
Candace: Are you saying that it would have been better if I had said, "I need to spend some time with you right now"?	+ Clarifies his request. + Looks for reassurance that he means what he's saying.
David: Possibly. I think you were trying to help me get my work done when that's not really what you wanted. You didn't want me to do this massage as just another part of my routine, just another one of my obligations. And I keep telling you, you're not just another obligation.	+ Shows he understands her feelings. + Encourages her to ask for what she needs, even if it's not convenient for him.
You want to feel important, like you're number one. And I want to make you number one. This morning, if you had told me honestly that that you needed to have an emotional connection—instead of expressing it as you did—then I think I would have reacted differently. Does that make sense?	+ Tells her she's important to him. + Expresses his willingness to be influenced by her. + To connect, asks for her validation.
Candace: It makes a lot of sense.	+ Validates his attempt to connect.

What They Say	What We Notice
David: After I made the phone calls and you said, "Well, it's not important. I don't need it now," I felt bad, because then I realized that the massage wasn't something that you wanted me to just schedule in.	+ Talks about his feelings, expressing his regret that he didn't meet her needs.

(Now it's Candace's turn to talk while David listens.)

What They Say	What We Notice
Candace: I need to know from you that I am number one. I would like you to do that almost automatically. Instead of putting me in the schedule when I ask you to, I would like you—all on your own—to say, "Let's spend a little time together." I need for you to just be sweet and romantic. You know?	+ Clearly states what she wants—for him to initiate time for connection, not just respond to her.
I like to be touched. And when I'm stressed, or when I'm grieving, or when I have a problem and I need to explain things to you, I need you to physically touch me.	+ Clarifies what she means by "sweet and romantic"; i.e., she states specific need for physical affection.
David: Do you think that's something I don't do enough of?	+ Asks for more information.
Candace: It's just what I need.	+ Sticks with her statement of needs. − Still avoiding conflict by not saying, "Right. You don't do it enough."

continued

49

What They Say	What We Notice
David: OK.	+ Good feedback.
Candace: I need you to listen to me, but mostly to touch me. Rub my skin. It makes me feel loved. It makes me feel that you're paying attention to me. *(She tears up.)*	+ Goes deeper, telling him about her most intense needs and feelings. + Her willingness to share tears gives her communication emphasis (like writing something in italics).
David *(sweetly)*: I understand that. You wish that I would anticipate those things more frequently.	+ Expresses his understanding by reflecting back what he hears.
Candace: That's true.	+ Affirms that he gets it.
David: That's a common complaint, I think. That you say, "Why don't you just think of this yourself? Why do I have to tell you?" That kind of bothers me. That you believe I should automatically think of these things. Is there a way to resolve that?	+ Expresses that he understands. + Expresses his complaint. + Shares responsibility for finding a solution. − May be slipping into problem solving a little too early.
Candace: I guess I just want you to know me well enough to know some of the things that I like. I'd like you to know me that well. *(She chokes up again.)*	+ Sticks with expressing her need. + Expresses her deepest need: for David to know her so well he understands what she needs.

What They Say	What We Notice
David: So that when I see you're under a lot of stress, that I would touch you more, or rub your shoulders, or give you a massage, or whatever.	+ Clarifies her need, showing that he understands. + Shows that he accepts her influence.
Candace: And it really irritates me when I see you taking care of everything else, when I haven't been taken care of. That bothers me.	− Misses the chance to acknowledge him for understanding. + Continues to go deeper, courageously expressing her anger as well as sadness.
David: Yeah. But when you're feeling that way, I need to know somehow. Maybe we can work out some kind of signal.	+ Expresses his need to be reminded. + Expresses willingness to find a solution together.

This time around, Candace has done a better job of expressing her needs, and David is much less likely to brush aside her concerns with premature reassurances. We got the sense that he was willing to stay with Candace as she talked about her sadness and her longing. This willingness allowed Candace to go deeper, which is essential to building a stronger bridge of emotional intimacy in the marriage. It's conversations like this that allow people to feel that their partners know and understand them.

In our session after this conversation, Candace talked more about wanting David to anticipate her needs *without being told*. This raises questions common to many couples in conflict: Is it fair to expect your partner to "read your mind"? Should your partner "automatically" know that you want a massage, a gift, a compliment, or sex? Unless

51

your partner is telepathic, it might be hard to guess what you need moment by moment, so how could such mind-reading possibly work? And yet some people feel that having to ask for affection or sex takes all the romance out of it.

Our response is to encourage couples to look at the longing behind their dilemma. What Candace craves, and what most people long for, is to know that they are a top priority in their partners' lives. They want to know that they are not just another obligation, another "duck" to line up in a row. (This is especially important to Candace because during David's affair, she was *not* number one.)

While Candace can't get David to read her mind, she can expect him to make a conscious effort to place a high priority on her needs and desires. By paying close attention, he might notice when she's feeling down and acknowledge that. He might think of her during the day and come up with expressions of affection to delight her. This could be a phone call "just to say hi," a quick note via e-mail, or an unexpected kiss. He might simply ask her from time to time, "Candace, what do you need from me?" If he does these things out of his own initiative—and not because Candace is asking for them—his efforts can go a long way toward healing their relationship.

In this second conversation, David does a much better job of responding to Candace's feelings. But there's still a big piece missing—discussion of *David's* needs. Noticing this, Julie quizzes David about his omission: "I know you need Candace to tell you what she wants, but where is David in all of this? Don't you need anything from Candace? Do you need her to touch you? Do you need to share your feelings with her? Do you need her to listen to you while you tell her how it felt to lose $50,000?"

"Yeah," David answers quietly. "I need that, too. And that was the problem back when I lost the money, when I had the affair."

"When it was your turn to speak about your needs, you asked Candace to let you be a better listener," says John. "But what do you, David, need directly?"

"I haven't thought about that too much," David answers.

This isn't surprising. Like many men in our culture, David has learned to ignore his emotions and focus instead on problem solving and accomplishment. So when his wife brings up difficulties in their relationship, his first instinct is to analyze the problem quickly as she presents it and to seek the solution. David successfully resisted this inclination in the second conversation. But he draws a blank when we say, "Tell Candace how *you're* feeling. Tell Candace what *you* need emotionally."

He's aware of feelings of "stress" related to his relationship with Candace, but it's just a vague sense of negative stimulation going on inside. He has no language to express it.

"Maybe I need to just say what I'm thinking," David offers.

"That would be a good place to start," Julie responds. "Take your thoughts and broadcast them. Make them external, rather than just hearing them on the inside. The expression of emotions will come eventually."

Julie also advises him to pay attention to physical sensations that come up. "Do you feel tension in your throat? Your chest? Your stomach? Is that physical sensation a sign of sadness? Anger? Fear? Once you start to get a handle on this, tell Candace what you're noticing. Say, 'When we talk about this, I feel this tightness in my throat.'"

Such simple statements could be a window into David's emotional life, a way for Candace to know that he needs her comfort and understanding. That gives her something she can respond to. Also, Candace can help by occasionally asking David, "What are you thinking? What are you feeling? What do you need from me right now?" After twenty-three years together, it can be challenging to find new ways to grow closer. But such exchanges could open new doors.

Candace and David leave the lab knowing they have a lot of work ahead, a lot of healing to do. But their shared affection and commitment to strengthening their marriage is evident. We believe it will see them through.

One Year Later

Candace and David both report they've made major improvements—especially at expressing what they need. And David is getting much better at listening to Candace; he's less likely to cut her off with empty reassurances.

"Rather than just trying to smooth things over, we're actually listening and talking to each other," says David.

This, in turn, means that Candace doesn't get emotionally flooded as easily and she's less likely to withdraw from the conversation.

Candace says she still wishes David would be more passionate, more romantic. She would like more spontaneous expressions of affection from him. And David agrees he could do more to meet Candace's expectations. But, overall, both say they're feeling less lonely in their marriage, more in sync.

"On a scale of one to ten, our marriage used to be a four or five," says Candace. "Now I'd say we're at about nine."

THE HAZARDS OF
AVOIDING CONFLICT

For most of their twenty-three years together, David and Candace had the type of relationship we call a "conflict-avoiding marriage." In such marriages, spouses would rather sidestep disagreements than explore conflicts and the potentially difficult emotions that might surface. If they find themselves in opposite corners over an issue, they're most likely to "let it go." Rather than argue, they say things like "Let's just agree to disagree."

There was a time when relationship experts believed that conflict-avoiding marriages were fraught with trouble. They believed that unless partners consistently aired their grievances and worked out their conflicts, the marriage would be unstable. But research we conducted in the 1980s comparing various styles of marriage proved this wasn't true. We learned that as long as both partners were comfortable sidestepping difficult issues, conflict-avoiding marriages could be just as stable as marriages where partners faced their problems head-on. Conflict-avoiding couples can get by for years, simply by ignoring or minimizing their differences. Some problems in these marriages get resolved by "letting time take its course"; other conflicts never go away. Still, these couples stick together, finding happiness in their basic shared philosophy of marriage. They reaffirm what they love and value in their relationships, accentuate the positive, and accept the rest. This allows them to bump into areas of disagreement, resolve very little, and keep feeling good about each other.

But there are some distinct dangers to this emotionally distant style of marriage. One is that partners don't get to know each other as well as couples do when they are more open to exploring their emotional differences. They're more apt to keep quiet about their dissatisfactions and their unmet needs. Some may develop a secret "inner life" that they keep from their partners. And if they meet someone outside the marriage with whom they can share this hidden side, they may be at risk for an extramarital affair.

The hazards of a conflict-avoiding relationship often become apparent when couples face crises such as serious illness, a death in the family, job loss, or acute financial trouble. In the midst of such life-altering experiences, people need a blueprint for talking through feelings of grief, sadness, or anger, and finding comfort in their relationships. Couples who have habitually sidestepped such tough feelings may lack such a blueprint. Consequently, crises cause them to become even more emotionally distant from each other. They begin to live parallel lives, sharing the same space, but never interacting in meaningful ways. Couples in these circumstances often report feeling terribly lonely in their marriages. And some turn to sexual relationships outside their marriages for comfort and support.

That's what happened to David and Candace. Their conflict-avoiding style of marriage served them well for twenty years—until David's financial problems upset their world. Unaccustomed to sharing his troubles with Candace, he turned instead to a coworker for understanding. And in an emotionally charged atmosphere of secrecy and grief, he stepped over a line he never intended to cross; he became intimate—first emotionally, and then physically—with somebody other than Candace.

How can conflict-avoiding couples steer clear of such risks? We recommend they learn to share strong emotions like anger, sadness, and fear with each other rather than suppress them. We advise couples to practice telling each other what they are feeling and what they need—even if such expression brings conflicts to the surface, where they have to be acknowledged and managed.

We recognize this may be a struggle. Some people, like David, have trouble identifying what they're feeling, so they find emotional expression very difficult. The exercise on page 65 ("Identifying Your Feelings") may help.

Others may feel uncertain about the way their partners might react to negative expressions of emotion or strong statements of need. The exercise called "Give Me a Clue" in chapter 9 might give you some insights. And some may fear that negative emotions, if expressed, will result in escalating arguments that spin out of control and endanger their marriage.

If you're struggling to face conflict in your marriage, you may find the courage you need if you

* Focus on the long-term well-being of your relationship. Learning to express feelings, state needs, and address conflicts will help to build intimacy and strengthen your relationship so that it can weather hard times. If you learn to do this under everyday circumstances, you'll have that blueprint in place when you face the major crises that inevitably come up in everyone's life.

* Try discussing conflicts using the mediation exercise developed by social theorist Anatol Rappaport, which is described in the chapter 9 section called "A Blueprint for Handling Conflict."

* Keep in mind that you can get help from professional counselors or clergy if it seems as though problems are getting out of hand.

* Reaffirm the strengths of your relationship as you work through conflicts. This can be done by asking each other such questions as these:

  1. *What values do we share about the importance of our relationship?*

  2. *What do we believe is a fair way for couples to settle their differences?*

  3. *Can we identify other couples we both admire who have solved tough problems in their marriages? If so, what can we learn from their marriage?*

* Keep your expectations for happiness in your marriage fairly high. If you and your spouse expect to feel fulfilled and satisfied with your relationship, you'll be more motivated to work toward that standard.

THE AFFAIR-PRONE MARRIAGE

Before David's affair with a coworker, he and Candace would have described their marriage as happy. That's not surprising. Although research shows that people dissatisfied with their marriages are more likely to stray than those who are content, a happy marriage is no guarantee against extramarital affairs.

Research also points to certain characteristics that are most often linked to infidelity. Some of these factors have to do with the individual. Being raised in a family where having affairs is considered normal is one example. Having the type of personality that values excitement and risk taking over marital stability is another. Your social environment also has a big impact. If you're surrounded by coworkers and friends who believe that affairs are OK, you're less likely to stay true to your partner. The nature of your marriage is an important factor as well. People who feel emotionally distant from their spouses are more likely to look outside the marriage for a sense of closeness.

In her book *Not Just Friends* (The Free Press, 2003), marriage researcher Shirley P. Glass presented a compelling description of the way many happily married people unwittingly make their marriages vulnerable to affairs. The problems often start when coworkers form secret emotional attachments to each other by crossing small boundaries that are needed to protect their marriages.

"One way to determine whether a particular friendship is threatening is to ask, *Where are the walls and where are the windows?*" Glass wrote. "In a committed relationship, a couple constructs a wall that shields them from any outside forces that have the power to split them up. They look at the world outside their relationship through a shared window of openness and honesty. The couple is a unit and they have a united front to deal with children, in-laws, and friends. An affair erodes their carefully constructed security system. It erects an interior *wall of secrecy* between the marriage partners at the same time that it opens a *window on intimacy* between the affair partners. The couple is no longer a unit. The affair partner is on the inside, and the marital partner is on the outside."

Glass said keeping track of walls and windows can help you determine whether an outside relationship is a potential threat. "When a friend knows more about your marriage than a spouse knows about your friendship, you have already reversed the healthy position of walls and windows," she wrote.

By describing it this way, Glass not only shows how natural it is for people to get caught up in extramarital affairs, she also shows that it's possible to recover from an affair and/or to make you marriage affair-proof.

Couples in conflict-avoiding marriages like David and Candace's may be especially prone to affairs, according to Glass's analysis. That's because when something occurs in a conflict-avoiding couple's life that raises new issues (i.e., a baby is born, or one spouse is stressed at work), the partners keep from expressing difficult feelings or stating new needs in order to "keep the peace." But this lack of sharing can cause one or both partners to feel lonely. Meanwhile, the lonely partner may happen to have an intimate or exciting conversation with somebody outside the marriage. This partner may know on a gut level that they should let their spouse in on this development and the feelings it brings up. They could say something like "I had the most intense conversation with Chris at the office today. And it made me realize that you and I haven't talked like that in a long time, and that worries me." But, as we all know, a revelation like this may lead to a heated argument—something the conflict-avoiding couple wants to avoid at all costs. So the lonely partner puts off discussing the situation. And as a result, he or she now has *a secret*. As Glass would put it, the walls and windows in this marriage have been reversed and a boundary has been crossed—and that's just the beginning.

This is exactly what happened to David and Candace. When David began confiding in his coworker about the way he had secretly lost the retirement funds he and Candace shared, he constructed a wall of secrecy between himself and his wife. At the same time, he opened a window of intimacy with his coworker. She now knew more about the current state of David's marriage than Candace did. And Candace knew nothing about David's new relationship at work. It was the perfect setup for an extramarital affair.

Once Candace discovered the affair and confronted David, however, the dynamics changed. He realized that he didn't want to lose his marriage. So he did exactly what Glass recommended. He ended the affair and cut off all contact with the woman at work. Now he and Candace were back together again, behind that secure wall of intimacy that marriage should create, and the coworker was on the outside, where friends and acquaintances belong.

Breaking off the affair, however, was not enough to heal David and

Candace's marriage completely. According to Glass, the betrayal and deception that usually go along with an extramarital affair can create a post-traumatic stress reaction in the betrayed partner. To help this partner heal from the trauma, the couple needs to do a great deal of talking. The partner who had the affair needs to patiently answer all of his or her spouse's questions about the extramarital relationship—how it started, how it was maintained, and what it meant for their marriage. While such discussions are difficult, Glass's research shows they're essential to helping betrayed partners cope with the trauma and loss of trust inherent to infidelity.

For David and Candace, talking about the affair was painful, but it helped them to create a window of emotional intimacy from which they can view the shared circumstances now affecting their marriage.

Couples who want to heal the damage that affairs create usually benefit from working with a marriage counselor. In fact, several studies have shown that marital therapy can be quite effective in helping couples to recover from an affair. Researchers David Atkins and Andrew Christensen found that while couples who have experienced infidelity typically start therapy in a more unhappy state than other distressed couples, they also make quicker gains over the course of six months with a therapist.

Our own work has shown that shared therapy can create a safe space for the betrayed partner to express pain and get the answers he or she needs. At the same time, a trained therapist can steer that partner away from expressions of rage that would be harmful to their relationship. The therapist can also help the couple avoid "the Four Horsemen," that is, the four types of emotional expression that our research has proven to be dangerous in marriage—criticism, defensiveness, contempt, and stonewalling.

Instead, the couple focuses on communication that helps to rebuild feelings of fondness and admiration. Partners may be encouraged to say why they want to stay in the marriage, what they once admired and still love about each other. They can work on getting to know each other in a more emotionally honest way. This, in turn, eliminates one factor that puts marriages at risk for affairs—emotional distance.

Quiz: Do You Avoid Conflicts, or Do You Talk About Them?

Although our research shows that conflict-avoiding marriage can be a stable marriage, it can also lead to emotional distance, which sometimes puts couples at risk for affairs.

This list of questions can help you determine whether you (Partner A) and your spouse (Partner B) are more likely to avoid conflicts in your marriage or to talk about them.

PARTNER A   **PARTNER B**
T/F   T/F

_____ 1. I often hide my feelings to avoid hurting or inconveniencing _____
          my spouse.

_____ 2. When we disagree, there's not much point in analyzing our _____
          feelings and motivations.

_____ 3. Time takes care of most of our conflicts.   _____

_____ 4. When I'm angry, I prefer to be left alone until I get over it. _____

_____ 5. During a disagreement, there's not much point in trying _____
          to figure out what's happening on a psychological level.

_____ 6. I think it's usually inappropriate to show strong signs of _____
          anger, sadness, or fear.

_____ 7. I just accept the things in my marriage that I can't change.   _____

_____ 8. We've learned not to talk about issues that cause _____
          disagreements.

_____ 9. Talking about disagreements just makes matters worse.   _____

_____ 10. There are some areas of my life that I prefer not to discuss _____
           with my partner.

continued

PARTNER A		PARTNER B
T/F		T/F
____	11. There's not much point in trying to persuade my partner to see things my way.	____
____	12. Thinking positively solves a lot of marital issues.	____
____	13. Anger doesn't solve anything.	____
____	14. I prefer to work out negative feelings on my own.	____
____	15. In our marriage, there's a fairly clear line between the man's role and the woman's role.	____
____	16. We turn to our basic religious or cultural values for help resolving conflict.	____
____	17. It's hard for me to show when I'm angry, sad, or afraid.	____
____	18. Expressing negative feelings is selfish; it just brings your partner down.	____
____	19. Expressing sadness, anger, or fear makes you appear weak and ineffective.	____
____	20. The best way to get over negative feelings is to ignore them until they go away.	____
____	21. We hardly ever disagree.	____

SCORING. Count the number of items you and your partner marked as "true." If either of you scored eight or more, you may prefer a style of marriage that avoids conflict.

If one or both of you find you prefer this style, you may need to work harder at staying emotionally close and guard your relationship against extramarital affairs.

Recognize also that you may face conflicts that simply have to be addressed. When this happens, the mediation exercise described below has proven especially helpful for people who would just as soon not fight.

Exercise: Calm Down to Avoid Flooding

Like many people, David and Candace often experience "flooding" when they're emotionally upset. That is, their bodies release stress hormones into the blood, causing their breathing rates to increase and their hearts to race faster. It's all part of the "fight or flight" alarm system that we human beings inherited through evolution to mobilize our bodies to react in emergency situations.

Although flooding may be a natural response to stress, it's rarely helpful in marital interaction. In fact, research links the tendency to flood under stress with higher rates of marital distress and divorce. For example, in one of our studies comparing couples who divorced with those who stayed married, husbands in the divorcing couples have heart rates that are 17 beats per minute higher than those of their counterparts in stable marriages.

Flooding makes it harder to think, listen, and communicate effectively. One partner may fail to hear the other's attempt at humor or reconciliation, for example. Flooding also gets in the way of empathy or creative problem solving. It can cause people to feel "out of control."

To avoid such problems, many couples steer clear of stressful conversations altogether. They don't talk about conflicts or difficult emotions that come up in their relationships. But conflict avoidance can lead to emotional distance and loneliness, which isn't good for relationships, either.

An alternative is to develop a ritual of taking breaks when one or both of you are upset. This ritual can help you to calm down and to cope creatively with conflict rather than run away from it. Here are some tips for developing a ritual that works for you:

1. NOTE PHYSICAL SENSATIONS THE NEXT TIME YOU AND YOUR PARTNER EXPERIENCE CONFLICT. Do you feel tension in your jaw, forehead, neck, shoulders, or other parts of your body? Does your breathing become faster or shallower? Are you finding it difficult to concentrate on what your partner is saying? Is your heart beating faster than normal?* These feelings may be signs that you are flooding.

---

* In general, a rate over 100 beats per minute indicates that a person's heart is racing too fast for assimilating information and communicating effectively. An athlete's limit is typically lower—about 80 beats per minute.

2. SUGGEST TAKING A BREAK WHEN YOU'RE FLOODING. Do this without blaming or judging. See it as part of a positive solution. Over time you may develop a simple word or signal that communicates, "Let's take a time-out" in a thoughtful, caring way.

3. SET A SPECIFIC TIME TO RETURN TO THE ISSUE THAT'S CAUSING DISTRESS. Your break should last at least twenty minutes, because that's how long it takes for the body's nervous system to recover from the release of stress hormones. Agree with your partner on a time to resume talking. Don't postpone your discussion indefinitely; that can just lead to more distress farther down the road.

4. DURING YOUR BREAK, DO SOMETHING YOU FIND SOOTHING. Go for a walk, take a hot bath, or do some gardening, for example. Or you may want to practice these steps to self-soothing:

- Focus on your breathing. Take several breaths, inhaling and exhaling deeply and evenly. Your stomach should expand when you breathe in, and contract when you breathe out.

- Scan your body to find areas of muscle tension. Consciously make those areas more tense, hold the tension for a moment, and then relax.

- Imagine those relaxed muscle areas as heavy.

- Imagine those relaxed, heavy muscles as warm.

- Now that your body is relaxed, visualize an image or idea that makes you feel calm.

5. AVOID DISTRESSFUL THOUGHTS ABOUT YOUR PARTNER DURING THE BREAK. Repeating statements in your mind like "I don't have to take this from him," or "Why does she always do this to me?" will keep your stress level elevated and won't help you to calm down.

6. ONCE YOU'RE SURE YOU FEEL CALMER, GET BACK TOGETHER WITH YOUR PARTNER AND TALK ABOUT THE CONFLICT IN A RESPECTFUL, ATTENTIVE WAY.

Exercise: Identifying Your Feelings

Sharing emotions doesn't come easily for some people—especially if they've been raised to ignore or discount feelings. Even those who *want* to tell their partners how they're feeling may discover they can't find the words.

We advise people to start by paying attention to physical signs of emotion in their bodies. The next time you're in an emotionally charged situation—an argument, for example, or a conversation when your partner is expressing a great deal of sadness—ask yourself these questions:

- What physical sensations am I feeling right now?

- Do I feel tension or discomfort in my jaw, throat, neck, chest, or other part of my body?

- Is there an emotion linked to this feeling? Is it anger? Sadness? Fear?

- What can I say to my partner about what I'm experiencing right now?

What you say can be as simple as "I feel very angry right now." And what if you're not certain about what you're feeling? You can express that, too. You can say, for example, "I'm not sure what I'm feeling, but I get this tight feeling in my chest when we talk about this."

Below is a list of words you can use to express what you're feeling. Some people in our workshops have found it helpful to write words like these on index cards and thumb through them when they're feeling strong emotions. In this way, they can find just the right word to express emotions, whether negative or positive. If you have trouble identifying the exact negative emotion, start with the word *upset,* and for positive emotions start with the word *good.*

NEGATIVE FEELINGS

sad	bored	fed up	fearful
crabby	put down	bitter	disgusted
grouchy	ashamed	restless	bewildered
anxious	guilty	trapped	puzzled
nervous	sorry	confused	upset
angry	frustrated	tired	

POSITIVE FEELINGS

happy	peaceful	grateful	joyful
stimulated	connected	centered	calm
warm	intrigued	appreciated	thrilled
loving	excited	energized	content
relaxed	strong	confident	loved
sexy	good		

Exercise: The Marital Poop Detector

David and Candace admitted that they tried to keep expectations for their marriage "realistic" as they grew older. This may have been a mistake. Research shows that people with the highest expectations for marriage usually wind up with the highest-quality partnerships.

One way to hold your marriage to high standards is to assess regularly how things are going. That way, you can detect small problems before they grow into big ones.

The following questionnaire, which also appeared in John's book *The Seven Principles for Making Marriage Work* (Crown, 1999), has proven to be a great tool for helping couples to do just that. We call it "the marital poop detector" because it helps you to sniff out problems at the first sign of trouble.

We recommend that you think about these statements often. Check as many as you believe apply. If you check more than four, plan to discuss these issues with your partner sometime within the next three days.

1. I have been acting irritable lately.

2. I have been feeling emotionally distant.

3. There has been a lot of tension between us.

4. I find myself wanting to be somewhere else.

5. I have been feeling lonely.

6. My partner has seemed emotionally unavailable to me.

7. I have been angry.

8. We have been out of touch with each other.

9. My partner has little idea of what I am thinking.

10. We have been under a great deal of stress, and it has taken its toll on us.

11. I wish we were closer right now.

12. I have wanted to be alone a lot.

13. My partner has been acting irritable.

14. My partner has been acting emotionally distant.

15. My partner's attention seems to be somewhere else.

16. I have been emotionally unavailable to my partner.

17. My partner has been angry.

18. I have little idea of what my partner is thinking.

19. My partner has wanted to be alone a lot.

20. We really need to talk.

21. We haven't been communicating very well.

22. We have been fighting more than usual.

23. Lately, small issues escalate.

24. We have been hurting each other's feelings.

25. There hasn't been very much fun or joy in our lives.

CHAPTER 3

"After All the Crises in Our Lives, We Don't Feel Close Anymore"

Mike and Maria arrive at the Love Lab exhausted. Parents of eighteen-month-old Tess, the Southern California couple has endured a litany of stressful events over the past two years. Maria's sister died from a complicated illness just six weeks before Tess was born. Then Mike, forty-three, was diagnosed with a heart defect that required open-heart surgery. Now Maria, thirty-nine, is struggling with a demanding new job as an officer for a financial services company. And Mike has the pressure of making a profit with his newly opened restaurant—a business he financed with investment from friends.

Reviewing the couple's questionnaires, we see that their lives are long on drudgery and short on fun. They have big concerns about their health because each has recently gained more than fifty pounds. Both have snoring problems, made worse by their weight gain, so they're sleeping in separate rooms. Feeling exhausted and unattractive, they've lost their interest in romance. In fact, it's been months since they've even attempted to have sex.

But it hasn't always been this way. In fact, when we ask Mike and Maria to talk about the way they met ten years earlier, they become

What's the Problem?

- Mike and Maria are dealing with grief, stress, and exhaustion.

- They have a crisis-driven habit of keeping a lid on feelings.

- They need deeper emotional intimacy, more sharing.

- Overworking, overeating, no exercise, and no fun have resulted in weight gain, loss of energy, sex, and romance.

What's the Solution?

- Reprioritize! Make big lifestyle changes, not small ones.

- Take time for relaxation, exercise, and romance.

- Go deep. Talk about your feelings.

- Connect emotionally before trying to solve problems.

suddenly energized and animated. Maria's face seems to light up in a rush of vivid, happy memories.

"It was one of those beautiful Friday nights in July—the first night of a three-day music festival," she recalls. "A beautiful setting. Gorgeous weather. Great music floating all around." Having arrived with a group, she and a girlfriend spotted Mike across an outdoor venue crowded with fans. In a silly mood, the two women started a game of paper, scissors, rocks to determine who would make a play for Mike. "We were both so interested in this cute guy with nice, long legs," Maria remembers. "Then he turns and starts walking straight toward us through the crowd. I took it as a sign from God!"

Maria didn't know that Mike had arranged to meet a friend in her group who was standing right behind her. Nor did she know that Mike was married at the time—although unhappily. That's why he kept his distance that weekend. But seven months later, after Mike's divorce was final, he found Maria through a mutual friend.

"Our first phone conversation lasted three hours," Maria recalls.

"We decided to have dinner later that week, but we couldn't decide where," Mike explains.

70

"So he called me back three nights in a row and we talked for hours each time," Maria says. "There was so much to say, we never did decide on a restaurant."

"Finally, we just had dinner at Maria's place," says Mike, smiling broadly. "Great conversation. Great wine."

"And extraordinary sex," adds Maria with a sigh. "For many years. We had a wonderful sex life. We're very earthy, very sensual people. And that was such a big part of our initial attraction—which is why we miss it so much now."

So how can they get it back? The first step, we tell them, is to acknowledge the cumulative effect of all the stress—both good and bad—that they've been through recently. They've had a baby, started new jobs, and survived Mike's heart surgery. All the while, they've been grieving the death of Maria's sister, whom they dearly loved. Individually, these are huge events that can take a toll on any marriage. Happening all at once, the impact has been devastating.

From this discussion, Mike and Maria move almost immediately into their concerns about their physical health. They see how the stress of the past two years has kept them from exercising and taking care of themselves. "The health issue ties into all our other problems," Mike explains. "If we were feeling healthier, we'd have more energy and feel more attractive, which would aid our sex life considerably."

Maria agrees. But because they devote nearly all their energy to their jobs and their daughter, there's no time for exercise or recreation.

"We've talked about taking better care of our health, and we've made a lot of plans," says Maria. "But we don't follow through."

Because this issue seems to loom so large for them as a couple, we suspect that a discussion about it may reveal a lot about their relationship with each other. So we ask them to talk about it one more time.

What They Say	What We Notice
Maria: The real issue is our health. And I'm assuming that if we pay attention to that . . .	+ Immediately frames the issues as a team effort.
Mike: A lot of other things will fall into place.	+ Validates.
Maria: Exactly. Energy level. Feeling attractive to each other. When we work together on something, we not only get the work done, but we do enjoy it more.	+ More good teamwork, a bid to join him in feeling connected.
Mike: Maybe that's the key, then. Because a lot of time when I have tried to lose weight, I've tried to do it on my own. But it's like a smoker trying to quit when there's another smoker in the house.	+ Accepts the bid. − Starts looking for the solution ("the key") before they've talked about their feelings; it's too early for this.
Maria: I know. We certainly haven't intentionally sabotaged each other, but it hasn't been as easy as it could have been.	+ Accepts some responsibility for the problem. + Avoids blaming.
Mike: And it does kind of work that way, intentionally or not.	+ Also avoids blaming.

What They Say	What We Notice
Maria: Diet and food is a big deal. But the bigger deal for me is getting into the routine of exercise. How are we going to do that? I got the membership started at the Y, but how do I push back against all the other pressures—like work—so that I actually make the time to do it? Once I get into the routine and start it, I believe I can sustain it. But it's overcoming huge inertia to start doing it.	− Continues in problem-solving mode, but it's still too early. − Not sharing feelings first.
Mike: For me, too. The problem is, we come up with so many great ideas and never follow through with any of them.	+ Validating. + Starts to express the despair he really feels.
Maria: I know. That's what I want help on. How do we actually hold each other accountable without saying "gotcha"?	+ Acknowledges his feelings. + Expresses desire for teamwork without criticism. − Goes back to trying to solve the problem.
Mike: Right. Maybe we could all get up at the same time so we could work out at least every other day.	+ Validating. − Still focusing on problem solving without exploring feelings.
Maria: In the morning? I need to get in to work earlier than you do. Getting up at 5:00 a.m. to work out is possible, but probably not very likely.	+ Clarifying. − But starting to offer resistance. − Resisting this solution.

continued

What They Say	*What We Notice*
Mike: And my best time for working out is morning. Because I don't get home until seven at night.	– More problem solving.
Maria: You're not going to get to bed at a reasonable hour if you go to the gym then.	– Resisting this solution, too, contributing to a feeling of hopelessness.
Mike: Exactly. Nor is Tess. Nor are you, if we're trying to do it together. So how about if we get up in the morning and at least have breakfast together? Then you go to work, and I'll take Tess to the daycare at the gym.	– Trying to be creative, and still problem solving, even though it's not working.
Maria: Then I'd take her to the daycare in the afternoon again? I don't like that.	– Still more resistance.
Mike: Oh God. Could we do it alternating days?	+ Starts to express frustration. – But jumps right back into problem solving.
(Silence. They stare straight ahead, looking absent, tired, bored.)	– No feelings; no emotional connection.
Mike: Heck! I don't know how to solve that one. But I know exactly what you mean. We need to spend time with Tess. And it needs to be good time. Right now if we're coming home and we're dead to the world, it isn't a good time!	+ Expresses frustration over this seemingly impossible situation. + Expresses shared values.

Our Analysis: Stress Creates Emotional Distance and Hinders Romance

First, we tell Mike and Maria how remarkable they are. It's unusual to see so much respect and acceptance when couples are dealing with a frustrating situation like this one. Under similar circumstances, many couples fall into a trap of blame, criticism, and defensiveness. But Mike and Maria don't take that destructive path. Instead, their habits of listening and responding to each other with respect reinforce their solidarity. They've got a terrific friendship.

Still, this conversation reveals some real problems. "There was very little emotion when you talked to each other," John tells them. "I felt like I was watching two people who had just had an 'emotion-ectomy.' "

We also notice how they zero in on problem solving before they've discussed their feelings. Mike, especially, seems intent on immediately brainstorming solutions. But each time he offers an idea, Maria responds with reasons why it won't work. She's not being belligerent; she's just trying to be realistic. They both appear very tired, as well. That's not a great state of mind for generating creative solutions. So eventually they fall silent, as though dealing with this issue is just too much.

"That moment of silence illustrated your dilemma in a really dramatic way," John tells them. "You seemed to be coming to the realization that you can't find time to exercise unless you take time away from the other things you're most committed to—your jobs and your daughter. No wonder you feel stuck."

What's the answer? Only Mike and Maria can say. But this much we know: They're going to have to bring some new insight and new energy to their situation. And that insight and energy have to come from a place of deeper emotional intimacy, more sharing. They've got to tell each other how they feel about the difficulties they've been going through.

We ask them to consider—once again—all the upheaval they've had in their lives in the past two years: a new baby, a death in the family,

Mike's heart surgery, Maria's new job, starting a new restaurant, and so on.

We also explore their family history and how that colors their response to stress. One of five children from a troubled marriage, Maria describes herself as the highly competent middle child who always made certain that her siblings' needs were met. She was also the most gifted intellectually—a distinction that had its costs. "My father always said to me, 'Of those to whom much is given, much is expected,'" she remembers. The pressure motivated Maria to do well in school and at work, but it also felt like a burden.

"As a young person, you were asked to play the role of this shining hero who cared for everyone, this superstar who made the family look good," suggests Julie. "And when you keep trying to play that role today, it doesn't leave much room for expressing your own needs or taking care of yourself."

Meanwhile, Mike is feeling tremendous pressure as well. His best friends have invested their savings in his business, so he'd better make a go of it.

So here we have two people who love each other profoundly, going through an extraordinarily stressful period of their lives. But instead of talking to each other about the feelings they're experiencing—emotions of grief, fear, anger, anxiety, frustration, and more—they carry on with a calm, brave stoicism, as if major transitions have caused no ripple, nothing is amiss.

What's the result? Emotional distance, a loss of intimacy, and the death of passion. Mike and Maria have become terrific teammates—sharing the responsibility of caring for their daughter and supporting their household. But they have lost their identity as lovers.

We know that Mike and Maria have the capacity to connect emotionally. Their vivid memories of their dating relationship—with its long, heartfelt phone conversations, deep sharing, and passionate sex—tell us so. But because of all the crises and change they've faced in recent years, they've developed a habit of pushing their feelings aside.

Instead, they have focused squarely on solving the serious problems that each day presented, believing they had neither the time nor the inclination for long, heartfelt conversations.

What's more, those same stressful life circumstances have led to poor health habits—overworking, overeating, getting no exercise, and gaining weight at an alarming rate. Their situation—especially considering Mike's heart condition—is putting their marriage, and perhaps Mike's life, at risk.

Our Advice

"View this as a wake-up call," John tells Mike and Maria. "You're in a marital crisis and you've got to treat it like one. Now is the time to make big changes in your life, not small ones. If you don't, things are not going to get better in your marriage. They're only going to get worse."

Mike and Maria's primary problem is the need to connect emotionally on a regular basis. But to do that, they've got to clear away the obstacles. They've got to reprioritize their lives, making room for rest, relaxation, better physical health, romance—and, ultimately, sex. And they've got to do it now.

To help them accomplish this, we recommend a broad-based prescription of lifestyle changes:

1. *Set better boundaries on the job so you can work less and enjoy life more.*

2. *Schedule weekly two-hour "dates" away from your child, where you can talk one-on-one without interruption.*

3. *Schedule quarterly romantic getaways together, leaving your child with a relative or babysitter.*

4. *Get on a healthy food plan.*

5. *Start exercising regularly.*

6. *Get medical advice about your snoring so that you can sleep better.*

And because they're so obviously exhausted, we also recommend that they take a vacation alone together as soon as they possibly can.

"You're both committed to your work, but if you're burning yourselves out, you're not being creative," John advises.

"And you're both such devoted parents," adds Julie. "But that means you'll want to stay healthy to watch your child grow older. So it's absolutely essential that you take care of yourselves for her sake."

Mike and Maria's reaction to our advice is positive. "You've just signed our permission slips," says Maria. "I'll tell them, 'I can't be at the board meeting; I'll be digging my toes in the sand.'"

And, presumably, there will be time for long, heartfelt talks as well. To help Mike and Maria practice, we suggest that they try talking about their health issues once again. Only this time we suggest that they postpone the problem solving. Determining logistics, like who's going to the gym when, can come later. What's most important is for them to focus on sharing their deeper thoughts and feelings about the issue.

Maria suggests this won't be easy for her: "There's this fear of being overwhelmed, that I'm opening up Pandora's box, rather than just loosening the tension on a spring."

Julie acknowledges Maria's fear: "The emotion may feel like a tidal wave. But emotions also ebb. They wax and wane in a natural way. You don't have to be afraid of them."

"But if you try to suppress them," adds John, "you often end up with this low-level depression or irritability. You pay a price for it."

"For me, that price is overeating," Maria admits.

John suggests the reason that Mike may have difficulty talking about his emotional needs, as well. "Here Maria is providing for the family while your new business may or may not work. So you wonder, 'Where do I come off, talking about my needs?'"

"You've hit the nail on the head," says Mike. "This immense disparity in our income is very tough."

"But we're asking you to put aside that tendency to keep your feelings hidden," says John. "Because the only way to be present with Maria is to get real about what you need and what you feel. Staying hidden is causing you both to become emotionally disengaged. And it's robbing you of your romance, your sex, your passion. You've got to become more vulnerable. You've got to say what you need."

Mike and Maria agree, and the two begin a second conversation, starting with a discussion of how their weight is affecting their health.

What They Say	*What We Notice*
Mike: Looking in mirrors is rather painful.	+ Good disclosure of his feelings.
Maria: Oh, I know. It's like a science fiction movie.	+ Validating. + Humor helps.
Mike: With bad casting.	+ More humor.
Maria *(laughing)*: I know. It is all those feelings of being a failure and being disgusting and just thinking, "Where do I start?" The problem is so big. Literally. *(Laughs)*	+ Good disclosure of her feelings. + Humor continues.
Mike *(sighs)*: Well.	+ More expression of feeling, perhaps sadness, without words.

continued

What They Say	What We Notice
Maria: So it's that sense of hopelessness. Having tried a couple times before to really get serious about losing weight.	+ Empathizes with him, putting feelings into words.
Mike: I feel disgusted because I quit smoking. So I know I've got the willpower to nail it. And here it is again. You know? It's bloody ridiculous!	+ Reveals more feelings—disgust, frustration, anger.
Maria: So you just feel annoyed with yourself and disgusted.	+ Summarizes his feelings, showing that she's listening.
Mike: I'm just flat-out angry with myself. Because there's no way that I should have allowed myself to get back into this shape, excuses or not. You know? Because if there's anybody who should know the meaning of being in shape, it's me. It's me.	+ Expresses more feelings. + Takes responsibility for the problem.
Maria: I know. It is scary. I've tried to just tell myself that everything is fine now. "He's fixed. You know, he's not going to die." *(She starts to cry.)*	+ Validates his expression. + Opens up emotionally, revealing her own fears, deepening the intimacy.
Mike: I have to tell you, I have not been that sure. I have felt the exact opposite. I have felt that my time is limited. I've felt that I am not going to be around long. You know? Whether I fix the weight or not. And it scares the hell out of me.	+ Joins her in this deeper emotional space, telling her what he fears, establishing that they're on common ground.

What They Say	What We Notice
Maria: Yeah. And it scares me for ourselves. It really scares me for Tess.	+ Continues to join him in this deep emotional space.
Mike: It scares me for that reason, too. And it scares me for you. I can't imagine doing what you did—how you watched me go through that.	+ Continues sharing feelings. + Tells her he admires her.
(They talk about the way Maria and his friends supported him through his heart surgery.)	
Mike: I get freaked out about your health, your weight, too. Tess can't . . . I can't . . . afford to lose you.	+ Continues sharing feelings. + Corrects himself to make it an even more profound statement of love.
Maria: So in addition to fearing the ultimate— that we're going to die prematurely because of not taking care of ourselves—there's just the reduced quality of life that we experience right now.	+ Continues sharing, broadening the topic. − Intellectualizes a bit, probably because she feels the need to lighten up.
Mike: Ummhmm.	+ Shows he's listening.
Maria: It feels like a huge loss.	+ Strong statement of feeling. + Avoids blaming.

continued

81

What They Say	What We Notice
Mike: And that actually gets me angry sometimes. At both of us, I mean. Because, it's like, damn it, this is important!	+ Strong statement of feeling. + Accepts responsibility for problem.
Maria: Right.	+ Validates his feelings, accepts what he's saying.
Mike: This is important for us.	
Maria: I know, and I make myself last on the list.	+ Validates what he's saying. + Accepts responsibility for the problem.
Mike *(flip, joking)*: Don't do that!	+ Uses humor that expresses empathy for her dilemma.
Maria *(laughs)*: I never learned how to put myself first. I never learned how to make it OK that I wasn't taking care of everything and everyone else around me. *(In tears.)* So it feels like I'm shirking my duty.	+ Responds to his humor. + Good insight. + Strong expression of emotion.
Mike: Ummhmm.	+ Shows he's listening.
Maria: And there are things that are left undone.	+ Expresses her worry.

What They Say	What We Notice
Mike *(sweetly)*: You know, I figure there is always something that's going to be left undone. We ain't gonna die with clean underwear.	+ Reassurance that she does fine. + Humor.
Maria: I will. *(Laughs.)*	+ Accepts his humor and returns it.
Mike: Thanks. *(Laughs.)*	+ More healing humor.
Mike: I just so much want to see us get back to where we were. You know? We do have to make time for us.	+ Brings the conversation back to the central issue—their intimacy and their feelings about it. + Avoids blame.
Maria: I know. I just miss that feeling of—just being in your arms.	+ Loving expression of her own need.
Mike: Yeah. I miss it, too. It's so much a part of what we were. The thing I really miss is that sense at the end of the day that it's OK. It's OK now. You can go to sleep.	+ Matches that loving expression with his own, making a deep connection.
Maria: I just remembered something that you said years ago—that your favorite times of the day were waking up and falling asleep with me.	+ More profound, loving expression. + Shares a loving memory of him, which incidentally helps him to tell her how much she means to him.

continued

What They Say	What We Notice
Mike: They still are. They still are. Believe me.	+ He responds with a deep, loving statement.
Maria: And I really don't want you to feel that you can't talk about how you're feeling. I know that I've conveyed a lot of that. As if I was saying, "What the hell do *you* have to feel resentful for?" "What the hell do *you* have to feel slighted about? Suck it up. I'm pulling every wagon in this relationship, so shut up and be grateful." And I am sorry for that, Mike.	+ Invites him to keep sharing feelings. + Takes responsibility for her part in creating emotional distance. + Apologizes for hurting him in the past.
Mike: It's OK. It really is OK. I understand. I think I had a pretty good idea of where it was coming from.	+ Accepts apology. + Expresses understanding.

By the end of this conversation, we're all fairly astounded at the depth of intimacy Mike and Maria have achieved.

"Until today, I had always assumed we were so good at talking about the whole picture," says Maria. "But now I realize we can go much deeper—that's not something we grew up knowing how to do."

They start off with humor, which softens the way to self-disclosure of difficult emotions like shame, fear, anger, and longing. Their willingness to be vulnerable to each other pays off richly. By the end of this short conversation, they've not only rekindled lost passion, but they're also starting to heal old wounds.

"This is the pathway for getting back to romance, passion, sex, and intimacy," says John. "And the great thing is, you have all the skills you need to do this at any time." "You also have all the love you need," adds Julie. "It never went away; it was there all along. You just have to remember to go to your emotions. It's almost like you have to imprint it on your brain: Feeling distant? Isolated? Lonely? Go to emotion. Go to empathy. Go to feeling."

One Year Later

When we follow up with Mike and Maria a year later, it's obvious that they answered the wake-up call. They've made a number of positive lifestyle changes that are reflected in their relationship and their physical health.

First, they're spending more time together just relaxing. In fact, when an opportunity came up to buy a small beach cabin a few hours from their home, they jumped at it. Now they're getting away to their computer-free, cell-phone-free hideaway at least one weekend a month.

"I had to realize that I have one of those jobs that's never done, and my family is more important," says Maria.

Mike had to make some changes in his job, too. Now he's got a manager to cover the restaurant on the weekends he leaves town.

Usually, they take two-year-old Tess along, but sometimes she stays with Maria's mom—giving Mike and Maria more time for conversation and romance.

Maria and Mike have also been finding time to exercise regularly. Mike goes to the gym midmorning after taking Tess to daycare. He also takes long walks on weekends at the beach. Maria sometimes stops at the gym at the end of the day before she picks up Tess. But she's also does a lot more physical activities with her daughter—like bouncing on a small indoor trampoline or dancing along to a "run, hop, and march" video. When Maria walks on the beach, Tess often accompanies her in a backpack.

The result of all this increased activity? Mike has lost ninety pounds and Maria has lost seventy.

But perhaps the biggest burden they've released is their stoicism.

"The session with the Gottmans made us realize that we had been through an incredible amount of change all at once and we hadn't really adapted to it very well," says Mike.

Adds Maria, "Keeping a lid on our feelings helped us to maintain forward momentum in our lives, but there was a price to pay for not acknowledging the extent of our pain."

So now the couple is making a conscious effort to share their feelings about life events—past and present. They're also sharing more appreciation, affection, and trust.

"We're definitely having more fun, less drudgery," says Mike. And the romance? "It's returning," he reports.

How a Little Selfishness Can Help Your Marriage

All of us face major stress at some point in our lives—such challenges as a serious illness in the family, adjusting to parenthood, or a demanding new job. And most of us respond by giving more. After all, that's what we're taught. In a crisis, you step up to the plate. You do more than your share. You put others' needs before your own. Such tendencies are not only admirable; in many cases they're essential to a family's survival.

Things tend to get worse, however, when people adopt such crisis-mode behavior beyond the crisis—when they turn self-denial into a habit, when self-neglect becomes a lifestyle. As Mike and Maria experienced, ignoring the body's needs for physical activity, sleep, and a healthy diet results in exhaustion and illness. Overwork and continual self-sacrifice lead to resentment, emotional distance, and loss of sexual intimacy. So although it may sound crazy to people who value hard work and devotion to family, our advice is this: You need to be a little more selfish.

Taking time for physical activity is the great example. Mike and Maria firmly believed that their daughter's needs must come first, so spending time at the gym seemed frivolous. By skipping daily exercise, they could give that extra hour each day to Tess. Of course, during much of the time they spent with their daughter, they felt exhausted and out of sorts. And that's not the kind of parents they wanted to be. When they decided to take more time to themselves for exercise, however, the dynamic changed. Yes, Tess is now spending a bit more time in daycare, but now she's got a healthier, happier mom and dad— which is something every child needs.

The same principle applies to pursuits that bring you sheer pleasure—activities such as music, sports, crafts, gardening, or spending time with friends. When responsibilities mount, such "indulgences" are usually the first to go. But outlets like these can also be some of the most revitalizing. They provide you with the energy you need to navigate hard times.

So what's a good response when your partner says, "I'm going for a run," or "I want to practice the piano"? Try this: "Great! I'll watch the kids. And when you get back, I'll take my turn."

It's also important to make time for relaxation together as a couple. We suggest that parents plan a weekend getaway without the kids every few months. And we strongly recommend that couples plan "dates" at least twice a month—even if it's just to go to a pub or coffee shop for an hour or two.

The point is to plan for uninterrupted time together when you can reconnect. If you've been going through a particularly trying time with family or work issues, it helps to talk about that and how it's changing your perspective, making you feel. (See the exercise on page 93: "Keep Your Love Map Up-to-Date.") And if you find that you spend most of your time talking about the kids or your jobs, that's fine—as long as you each take the opportunity to share your feelings and be heard about the things that matter most in your lives. While such conversations are important at any time in your marriage, they can be especially valuable as you weather stressful periods or times of big transition. They allow you to stay in touch with each other.

That way, the storm brings you closer together instead of driving you apart.

Quiz: How Much Stress Have You Had Lately?

Evaluating how much stress they had recently experienced helped Mike and Maria see their marriage from a new perspective. Their problems weren't caused by a lack of love, or by a lack of trying. They had simply been overwhelmed by the pressures of a new baby, new jobs, Mike's illness, Maria's sister's death, and more. Once they acknowledged this, they felt motivated to make big changes to reduce stress and to take better care of themselves and their relationship.

The following test is a common one, developed by researchers Thomas Holmes and Richard Rahe to help people measure stress in their lives and to determine whether that stress might be putting them at risk for illness. Take this quiz with your partner to see how you score.

Keep in mind that people adapt to stress in different ways. Some have a high tolerance and don't seem to be bothered much physically or mentally by the kinds of events listed in the test. Other people can be very sensitive to stress, and they may experience negative effects at levels even lower than this test would indicate. The test is simply meant to show you how you might compare to the average.

If you have a high score (say, 300 or above) and your marriage is distressed, it may be that your relationship is not the source of your pain and unhappiness. Rather, your troubles could be based on an unfortunate set of circumstances you've been going through. Stress at high levels can erode your sense of perspective and interfere with good communication and emotional communication. If you think that might be the case in your marriage, talk over this list of stresses with your partner and take a critical look at your lives. Consider what you've both been going through, where you are now, and what you might want to do to reduce stress in the future.

"After All the Crises in Our Lives, We Don't Feel Close Anymore"

Circle those events you have experienced in the past year. Then total the number of points assigned to those items you've circled.

Event	Score
Death of a spouse	100
Divorce	73
Marital separation	65
Imprisonment	63
Death of a close family member	63
Major personal injury or illness	53
Getting married	50
Dismissal from work	47
Marital reconciliation	45
Retirement	45
Major change in health of family member	44
Pregnancy	40
Sexual difficulties	39
Gain of new family member (birth, adoption, elderly relative moving in)	39
Major business readjustment (merger, reorganization, bankruptcy)	39
Major change in financial state	38
Death of a close friend	37
Change to a different line of work	36
Change in number of arguments with spouse	35

continued

Event	Score
Major mortgage	32
Foreclosure of mortgage or loan	30
Major change in responsibilities at work	29
Son or daughter leaving home	29
Trouble with in-laws	29
Outstanding personal achievement	28
Spouse begins or stops work outside home	26
Beginning or ending formal schooling	26
Change in living conditions	25
Revision of personal habits	24
Trouble with boss	23
Major change in work hours or conditions	20
Change in residence	20
Change in schools	20
Major change in recreational activities	19
Major change in church activities	19
Major change in social activities	18
Minor mortgage or loan	17
Major change in sleeping habits	16
Major change in number of family get-togethers	15
Major change in eating habits	15
Vacation	13
Christmas season	12

Event	Score
Minor violation of the law (traffic ticket, etc.)	11

SCORING:

Less than 150 points = low risk of developing stress-related illness

150–300 points = medium risk of developing stress-related illness

More than 300 points = high risk of developing stress-related illness

Exercise: Steps to a Healthier Lifestyle

As Mike and Maria's story shows, taking care of your health is important to a happy marriage. But changing your habits around diet, exercise, work, and relaxation can be challenging. Mike and Maria's experience also shows that it *can* be done, however—especially if you attend to the emotional issues that may be keeping you from making self-care a top priority. Once those matters are addressed, you feel more motivated to follow through on basic advice for healthier living.

Research on behavior change shows that people who set goals, make a plan, and then track their progress have the most success. We recommend you consult with your personal physician on a regular basis, and especially if you're starting a new exercise program or food plan. If you're ready to make some positive changes, the following tips and questions may help:

Tips for Goal Setting

- *Make your goals specific.*
- *Make your goals measurable.*
- *Think about the pros and cons of making healthy changes.*
- *Break big goals into little ones.*
- *Ask for support.*
- *Anticipate obstacles and have a backup plan.*
- *Make a daily plan and track your progress.*
- *Reward yourself for short-term and long-term success.*

91

1. WHAT LONG-TERM GOAL WOULD YOU LIKE TO ACHIEVE? Think about it in a way that's *specific* and *measurable*. (*Example:* Don't say, "We need to talk more." Say, "Let's schedule a date every other Saturday morning. We'll use the time to go to the coffee shop and just talk. Then we'll go for a jog, or hang out together at the bookstore.")

_____

_____

2. MAKE A LIST OF PROS AND CONS OF ACHIEVING THIS GOAL.

Pros	Cons
Example: Regular dates will help us feel closer to each other.	*Example:* It will be expensive to hire a babysitter each week.

For each "pro" on your list, close your eyes and imagine achieving this benefit. For each "con," consider how you'd respond to a friend with the same concern.

3. WHAT SMALLER STEPS CAN YOU TAKE TO ACHIEVE YOUR LARGER GOAL? (*Example:* If your main goal is to "get in shape," smaller steps might be "Work out with weights for thirty minutes three times a week; run or swim for forty minutes two times a week.")

_____

_____

_____

_____

4. WHAT OBSTACLES CAN YOU FORESEE? HOW CAN YOU BREAK THROUGH OR GET AROUND THESE OBSTACLES? It pays to have a backup plan. (*Example:* If your goal is to exercise and you usually walk outdoors, think of what you'll do when the weather is just too lousy. Will you go to a gym? An indoor pool? Walk the mall?)

_____

_____

_____

_____

5. NAME THREE PEOPLE YOU CAN COUNT ON TO SUPPORT YOU IN THIS CHANGE.

1. _____

2. _____

3. _____

Contact them and ask for their encouragement. Call them when you need a boost.

6. HOW WILL YOU REWARD YOURSELF? Make a list of things you enjoy that also support your changes. Think of rewards for both short-term and long-term achievements.

- Rewards for meeting my one-week goal (*examples:* massage, lunch at my favorite restaurant, a music CD, flowers for my desk):

_____

_____

_____

- Rewards for meeting my one-year goal (*examples:* a trip to Mexico, season tickets, a week off to do whatever I want):

_____

_____

_____

_____

7. HOW WILL YOU KEEP TRACK OF HOW YOU'RE DOING EACH DAY?
Will you jot down notes on a calendar or in your Palm Pilot? How about a star on your calendar for each day you meet your goal? Would you find it helpful to keep a special journal related to this issue?

_____

_____

_____

Whatever method you choose, try to

- Review your goals daily, remembering the reasons you want to make changes.

- Decide on your intentions for the day. (*Examples:* "I'll stay away from the doughnuts at the staff meeting," or "We'll spend at least fifteen minutes of uninterrupted time tonight talking about our day.")

- Review what happened the day before: Were you successful at meeting your goal? What worked? What didn't? What could you do differently today to have more success? Use this information to revise your goals as needed.

Exercise: Keep Your Love Map Up-to-Date

In John's book *The Seven Principles for Making Marriage Work* (Crown, 1999), we introduce the concept of "love maps"—our term for the part of your brain where you store important information about your partner's life. These maps hold details about your partner's life history, daily routines, likes, and dislikes. Our research shows that couples who maintain accu-

94

rate and detailed love maps of each other's lives have happier marriages. They're also better prepared to weather difficult life passages, such as having a baby or losing a parent. Such important life events can change individuals' whole view of themselves and their place in the world. That's why it's especially important to keep your love maps up-to-date during times of transition. Doing so may allow you to grow closer during challenging periods rather than to drift apart.

Below is a list of questions to help you update your love maps. To benefit from this exercise after stressful or life-changing events, set aside some uninterrupted time when the two of you can take turns asking and answering these questions at a relaxed pace. As your partner searches for honest answers, do your best to listen and respond in an open and supportive way.

- How has this event (change, transition, loss, stress) changed how you feel about your life?

- How has it changed the way you feel about your role in your extended family?

- How has it changed the way you feel about your job?

- How have your priorities changed since this event occurred?

- How has it changed your views regarding religion, spirituality, or God?

- How has it changed the way your think about the future?

- How has it changed the way you think about serious illness or death?

- How has it changed your experience of time? Are you more concerned or less about what might happen in the future? Do you find you're paying more attention or less to things that are happening in the present moment?

- How has it changed your relationship with your friends or relatives?

- How has it changed what you need for yourself? (For example, are you less interested in material goods, more interested in emotional connection?)

- How has it changed your sense of security in the world?

- How has this affected your daily mood?

- What kind of support do you need from me as you enter this period of your life?

CHAPTER 4

"You Never Talk to Me"

Conversation wasn't a problem for Bob and Marilyn when they met at their small-town Iowa church in 1944. At age seventeen, Bob found fourteen-year-old Marilyn "very attractive, very jolly, and very talkative."

Whatever Bob didn't say during their wartime courtship, he conveyed in other ways. He came home on leave from the army with Marilyn's name tattooed on his arm.

"All of our dating was closely chaperoned," Bob remembers. "We'd sit on the front porch swing near the window with Marilyn's mother sitting just inside."

"She would pass by pretty often," recalls Marilyn. "Then she'd come to the door and say, 'All right, Marilyn, it's time to come in.'"

But one night before his leave ended, Bob borrowed a car from Marilyn's brother and took her out for a spin. Alone with Marilyn at last, Bob asked her to marry him.

"It took me about a minute to decide," says Marilyn. "I thought he was wonderful."

The couple wed shortly after the war, and had their first of three daughters one year later. For nearly their entire life together, they lived

What's the Problem?

- Bob and Marilyn criticize and insult each other.
- Each launches counterattacks of more criticism, more contempt.
- Over time, the marriage feels unsafe, so they withdraw and quit talking.
- Stonewalling and silence lead to more bad feelings, more criticism.

What's the Solution?

- Say "what I want" rather than "what I don't want."
- Resist the urge to respond with countercriticism, countercomplaints, or stating "what I want" in return.
- Instead, simply listen.
- Respond to criticism with the honest question, "What do you want?"
- Express appreciation to each other for listening and responding.
- Take steps to nurture positive thoughts and feelings about each other.

a sort of parallel existence. Marilyn was in charge of the kids, the household, and the family's social life. Bob focused on his sales career outside the home. With Bob's retirement, however, those lines have now intersected, and the adjustment has been hard.

Marilyn, now seventy-two, says her biggest complaint is that Bob won't talk to her. "Whenever I go out someplace, he always asks, 'What did you do?' And I used to tell him everything," she says. Recently, however, she noticed Bob doesn't do the same. "He comes home and I ask, 'How'd it go?' And he'll say, 'I golfed.' That's it. No detail. No communication. Nothing."

Feeling hurt, Marilyn decided, "That's not right. Why should I share the details of my life with him if he doesn't care enough to share his life with me?"

But Marilyn's not the only one feeling injured. "When I retired, it seemed like Marilyn took all the pent-up things she didn't like about me—and she dumped on me all at once," Bob, seventy-five at the time of our first interview, told us.

Marilyn agrees that Bob's retirement seemed like a turning point. "Now that we're together all the time, when I try to talk to him, he gets very defensive, very angry. I don't know how to deal with it."

"I get the feeling that she resents me being around," Bob says. "It's like I'm interfering, like I'm no longer needed."

It's not surprising that Bob and Marilyn's problems have come to a crisis at this point in their lives. Like other major transitions in a couple's life—the first baby, kids leaving home, and so on—retirement often brings marital difficulties into sharper focus. Problems that once seemed possible to ignore suddenly feel intolerable.

To better understand how Bob and Marilyn get along, we ask them to talk to each other about this problem they have talking.

What They Say	What We Notice
Bob: I'd like to know what you expect from me, as far as improving communications.	+ Asks her what she needs.
Marilyn: I'd like you to just plain talk to me—like you do other people. You just ask me questions. "What'd we get in the mail?" Or, "What's for lunch?" That's not communicating. It's not telling me how you feel.	+ Responds in a clear, specific way. – Slightly critical.
Bob: Yeah, but when I ask questions, you get resentful. Like when you get off the phone with your sisters, I ask questions because you never volunteer to say anything. I just want to be part of what's going on.	– Critical. – Defensive; takes no responsibility. – Globalizes the problem with "you never . . ." + States his need to be involved.

continued

What They Say	What We Notice
Marilyn: Well, when you're talking to someone, and I say, "What did they say?" you don't tell me. You say, "They were just talking." You don't tell me one thing.	− Counterattacks with a righteously indignant form of defensiveness.
Bob: I do, too. I tell you what happens on the golf course, how we got caught in the rain.	− Defensive; still taking no responsibility. − Not accepting influence.
Marilyn: You're mentioning one time when Fred was there. I'm talking about when we're alone. There's no communication, Bob. We go days without saying a word. If you go outside to work in the garage, and I say, "What are you doing?" You say, "Nuthin'." You make me feel shut out of your life totally. I don't know how you feel and I don't know how you think. The only time I know how you feel is when you become very angry at me. And I was—	+ Acknowledges that he did share some detail once. − Becomes defensive and critical again. − Imitation ("Nuthin' ") expresses contempt. + Complains in a specific way. + Tells him how she feels. − Criticizes him again at the end.
Bob: Well, I get angry because I know you're not listening to me. You start finishing my sentence and telling me what I'm thinking.	− Interrupts. − Countercriticizes.
Marilyn: But when you want to talk, you go on for ten minutes and I'm not supposed to say one word.	− Defensive. − Countercriticizes and ups the ante; she's unhappy that he doesn't express his feelings and that he talks too much when he does.

What They Say	What We Notice
Bob: You don't interrupt your sisters like you do me.	— Another criticism.
Marilyn: My sisters and I interact, Bob. With you, I'm supposed to sit and listen to you go on and on and on.	— Criticism and contempt.
Bob: Because I lose my train of thought when you interrupt me.	—/+ Although he's defensive, he tells her something important about himself.
Marilyn: Well, that's mutual.	+ Adds her own self-disclosure, shows they're in the same boat.
Bob: And when I do that, I get angry. Not at you, necessarily—just at my inability to express myself. A lot of the times you tell me, "That's stupid," when it may be stupid to you, but it's the way I wanted to express myself.	+ More self-disclosure. + Starts to try to repair the interaction. — Criticizes her, which interferes with his ability to repair.
Marilyn: And what about when I'm trying to express myself? You get angry at me and you get up in my face. And then you'll storm outside.	— Cross-complaint. — Defensive, critical.
Bob: That may be true, but I still don't like it. That's why I try to get away from it.	+ Some acknowledgment, taking some responsibility. + Tell her about his feelings; could repair the interaction.

continued

101

What They Say	What We Notice
Marilyn: I don't like it, either.	+ Expresses her feelings.
Bob: Well, me neither. I don't like to be called names.	+/− Still trying to repair, but turning back to criticism.
Marilyn: I don't like to be called names, either.	− Defensive. − Counterattacks.
Bob: I don't call you names, Marilyn.	− Defensive.
Marilyn: Bob . . .	− Defensive.
Bob: You *always* call *me* names.	− Escalates the criticism.
Marilyn: Please don't say that, because you *do* call me names.	− Defensive. − Critical.
Bob: Do you remember saying, "It's never going to change"? When you say that, I don't know where to go because it leaves no possibility.	+ Good switch to self-disclosure, letting her know how desperate he feels when she's so fatalistic.
Marilyn: Well, this has been going on our whole married life. And there have been times you've said, "I will change," but you don't. I'm willing to have closeness and companionship, but it's not there. I'm sorry, it's not there. I wanted it.	− Criticizes with global statements that go right to the heart of his fatalism. − Denies responsibility for their problems.

What They Say	What We Notice
Bob: I don't know how to change it, because I don't think you understand how I feel when you totally reject me by calling me names and telling me it's never going to change.	+ More self-disclosure. – Turns to criticism.
Marilyn: You keep talking about me calling you names, and—	+ A genuine inquiry; she wants to understand why he's saying this.
Bob: You do that. You call me a liar. You call me by my dad's name because you know it insults me. You don't understand what that does to me. It leaves me feeling that I'm totally unwanted. And I don't want to be rejected by the person I love. I could stand it from people in the world. But from the person that I love, it just does something to me on the inside. And I guess that's when I become angry, because I've—	– Interrupts her. + Specific complaints that lead to more description of how deeply hurt and rejected he feels. + Reveals his love for her, an attempt at repair that could have healing results.
Marilyn: You were angry before. And the last few years, I have tried to fight back. I thought, "I'll call you names, because you call me names."	– She counterattacks; his repair attempt fails.
Bob: What names have I called you?	+ A genuine inquiry; he's still trying.
Marilyn: You know.	– Bitterness.
Bob: No, I'm asking.	+ Stays with the inquiry. *continued*

103

What They Say	What We Notice
Marilyn: You have called me names for years.	− Criticism.
Bob: What names have I called you? I do not remember calling you names.	+ Stays with the inquiry.
Marilyn: You would say words that we were taught not to say.	−/+ Responds to his inquiry, but with veiled criticism, moralizing.
Bob: I wasn't calling you—	− Defensive.
Marilyn: What names am I calling you, then?	− Interrupts/defensive.
Bob: Well, you call me stupid.	+ Responds with specific complaint.
Marilyn: Well, you call me stupid, Bob.	− Defensive in a reactive way; not really taking in what he's saying.

Our Analysis: Attacks and Counterattacks Make the Marriage Unsafe for Conversation

Bob and Marilyn's conversation continues like this until we call a cease-fire and join them in the lab. "Was that similar to the kinds of discussions you have at home?" Julie asks as she takes a seat.

"Yeah," Bob answers sadly, and Marilyn nods. She looks sad, too, and it's little wonder. Both have said what they want from each other—somebody to talk to, somebody to listen, an end to all the painful insults and name-calling. But the trouble is, they've expressed their needs in extremely negative ways—by hurling criticism and accusations at each other.

To find out how these patterns developed in their marriage, we ask Bob and Marilyn to tell us a bit about their families. Bob describes his father as angry, judgmental, and unforgiving, and Marilyn chimes in.

"I think that figures into a lot of our problems," she says. "I can see Bob's dad in him and there are times when I tell him, 'I wish I never knew your dad. It might be easier that way.'"

"That must really hurt Bob when you say that," John offers.

"I'm sure it does," says Marilyn, "and I mean it because I usually say it when we're in a big, big fight."

Later on, we talk about Marilyn's development from a quiet young woman who was afraid to speak her mind, to someone who became quite vocal about her needs.

"How did that happen?" John asks.

"I don't know," Marilyn replies.

But Bob has an answer. "Marilyn has always been very aggressive, very domineering," he says with a wry chuckle. "The whole family knows it."

John observes that Marilyn might be insulted by Bob's remark, but Bob is not about to apologize. Instead, he says, "I know she would be insulted. I just don't understand why she doesn't see it."

Despite such hostility, however, Bob and Marilyn show a vulnerability and tenderness toward each other that makes us realize how much they want to change.

"I don't want to grow old and not have a secure, loving feeling," Marilyn tells us. "I want a relationship where, when you hurt, the other person knows it. And when you're happy, they'll know that too."

Bob reflects on better times, but seems to fear what may be in store: "If we can't somehow learn to relate to each other without being so hurtful, I'm afraid that all our joys in this life will be obliterated."

There's good reason for Bob to worry. Their conversation has demonstrated three of the four behaviors that we call "the Four Horsemen of the Apocalypse"—behaviors that almost always lead to the deterioration of marriages. Bob and Marilyn have shown us criticism, contempt, and defensiveness. As for the fourth horseman, stonewalling—that's what their whole conversation was about: the way they withdraw and refuse to share the details of their lives with each other.

For Bob and Marilyn to find a better way to relate, they'll need a deeper understanding of how they're hurting each other. So Julie asks them to reflect on what just happened.

"Bob, when you said Marilyn was aggressive, you kind of laughed about it," says Julie. "It may have felt like a joke, but that joke also expresses contempt—like you're putting yourself above her and trying to make her feel ashamed of herself.

"And likewise for you, Marilyn. When you say Bob is 'just like his father,' that strikes him as a putdown, an assault on the person he's trying to be in this world. That's very painful and he's asked you not to do it."

Over time, such attacks cause people to feel psychologically unsafe in their marriages. With so much criticism and contempt in the air, neither partner feels like talking about things that really matter to them. They don't share their goals, their dreams, or their regrets. Bringing up topics like these feels too risky; they know all too well anything they say can and will be used against them. We saw a clear example of this in Bob and Marilyn's first dialogue, when Bob tried to tell Marilyn how hurt and rejected he felt. This would have been a great moment to reward his vulnerability with compassion, but instead Marilyn used it as an opportunity to attack him again. When people experience this kind of hostility repeatedly in intimate relationships, they learn to clam up and keep their emotional distance. Eventually they stop sharing even the smallest details. It's a lonely way to live.

Our Advice

Bob and Marilyn need to stop this cycle of attacking each other and defending themselves with counterattacks. That's the only way they are going to make their marriage feel safer and move out of their isolation.

After more than fifty years of marriage, it's not easy to change patterns of interaction. Still, we've seen couples at all ages change their marriages for the better, and we believe that Bob and Marilyn can do it, too.

For starters, we ask them to consider these simple steps:

1. TELL EACH OTHER WHAT YOU *WANT* RATHER THAN WHAT YOU *DON'T WANT*

For example, instead of saying, "I don't want you to call me names anymore," try saying, "I want to feel as if you respect me. As if I'm your friend."

This is easier if you focus on the present, rather than the past. Don't concentrate on what your partner didn't do five years ago, five weeks ago, or even five seconds ago. Think about what you want from your partner in the moment.

2. RESPOND TO EACH OTHER'S STATEMENTS OF NEED WITH OPEN-ENDED QUESTIONS

This may take some extra thought, especially while you're trying to break old patterns. Just remember:

- *Don't jump in by stating your own need. ("Yeah, well, I'd like to feel respected, too!")*

- *Don't react defensively. ("Oh, so now you're saying we're not friends anymore!")*

Instead, try to *truly listen* and *understand* what your spouse is saying. You might ask questions like "What could I do that would make you feel more respected?" Or "This seems important; tell me what my friendship and respect mean to you."

If you should find yourself reacting in a defensive way, stop. Take a deep breath to calm down. Then start again, this time with a simple question, such as "Can you tell me more about this?"

3. Express Appreciation to the Spouse Who's Been Listening

Tell your partner when you feel you've been heard. Say, "Thank you for listening to me."

These three simple steps can be used under just about any circumstances when partners need something from each other. Whether you're expressing a need for companionship, sex, a balanced checkbook, or help with the laundry, the dynamics are the same. State your needs clearly in a positive way; practice careful, active listening through open-ended questions; and show your gratitude.

In Bob and Marilyn's case, we anticipate that this formula might give them new hope that loving, respectful conversations are possible again. We want to demonstrate that they can talk about their needs without feeling as though they've got to defend themselves against attack.

Bob and Marilyn agree to try our advice in their second conversation. They decide to start by discussing what they want from each other in everyday interactions, such as sharing the computer.

What They Say	*What We Notice*
Marilyn: When I ask, "Do we have any interesting e-mails from anyone?" I would like for you to say, "Yeah, we've got one here from so-and-so," or maybe read it to me. That would make me feel more like part of the computer thing, because I'm not as involved in it as you are.	+ Good start: explaining a specific need.
Bob: Would you like me to tell you when there's something in there you'd be interested in?	+ Genuine request for more information; not defensive.

What They Say	What We Notice
Marilyn: Yeah. Just say, "There's a message here from Bill." And when I'm at the computer, I'd like you to be more willing to help me out—show me the things that I forget to do.	+ Good response, focused on her specific need; avoids focusing on what he doesn't do for her.
Bob: Do you want me to do this at any particular time?	+ Asks for more information.
Marilyn: No, just when you're at the computer. I would like to know sometimes what you're doing.	+ Tells him more about what she needs.
Bob: I didn't know that you really wanted me to show you how to do it. And I appreciate you thinking that I might know something about it.	+ Expresses appreciation!
Marilyn: Well, yes. I feel like you know more about it. And when I'm trying to do my photos, just kind of help me along.	+ Acknowledges his competence; a compliment! + Explains more about what she needs.
Bob: I'd be glad to help you. Of course, I haven't gotten into the photo reproduction as much as you have. So I'm not sure about offering you instructions on something that you've been doing longer than I have.	+ Responds with willingness to help her. + Acknowledges her competence; a compliment!

continued

What They Say	What We Notice
Marilyn: Sometimes I forget things, and you can figure out what I've done wrong.	+ Tells him she needs him and that he's capable; another compliment.
Bob: I don't think you're doing things wrong. It's just that you learn by doing. But I'd be glad to offer information, as much as I can.	+ Reinforces his belief in her competence. + Expresses willingness to help.
Marilyn: I think it'd be more fun for us if we did it together. That'd make me feel more a part of your life.	+ Expresses optimism in their relationship. + Expresses her need to feel closer to him.
Bob: I think that's probably true.	+ He agrees with her optimism!
(They switch roles, talking about something Bob wants.)	
Bob: When we're planning to go somewhere, I'd like to get some idea of what you think needs to be done before we go. So then I can work within that framework.	+ Also a good start; expresses a need while avoiding criticism.
Marilyn: Um, I don't understand what you mean.	+ Asks for clarification; avoids defensiveness.

What They Say	What We Notice
Bob: Before we go to the city to the doctor or whatever, I'd like to know what you have in mind so I can do my things around that schedule. Sometimes I feel like I'm in limbo. I don't know whether to go start some project. And it would help if you could let me know what you need to do and what I can do.	+ Describes his need in a more specific way.
Marilyn: Well, I will try to be aware of that, but we both know what time our appointments are. And I feel like there are certain things that have to be done before you leave the house, and . . . and I don't know . . . maybe if you'll tell me the things that you need to do.	+ Expresses willingness to be aware of his need. −/+ Starts to get defensive, but then stops herself and goes into a problem-solving mode instead. Good save!
Bob: A lot of the time, I start moving things toward the car before you're ready for them to be packed. So if I could just get some general outline . . .	+ Gives her more detail about what he needs.
Marilyn: Well, I'll try to be more aware of that, to let you know the things that need to be done before we can leave	+ She agrees to meet his need.
Bob: I appreciate that.	+ A genuine, heartfelt appreciation!

continued

What They Say	What We Notice
Marilyn: I know it can be a real hassle some-times when we have doctors' appointments and a list a mile long. But it's something that we can work on together. I'll try to let you know what I have to do. I appreciate you thinking about it and wanting to make things better.	+ Acknowledges that they share the "hassles" of life together. + Expresses optimism in the relationship. + Expresses willingness to work together. + Expresses that she appreciates him!

When the dialogue is over, we rejoin the couple and John asks, "How did that feel, compared to your first conversation?"

"It felt better, like we were respecting each other's thoughts and ideas," says Bob.

Marilyn is impressed that they could make such an improvement just by discussing "small things" such as e-mail or setting out the luggage.

But this doesn't surprise us. "Here's the truth about marriage," says John. "It's the small positive things, done often, that make all the difference. You did everything right. You were saying what you need, you were asking good questions, you were expressing appreciation. These are things you have to keep in mind all the time. You have to do them as often as you possibly can. Doing so will prevent you from falling into criticism and contempt—which can destroy your relationship and make you very lonely."

At the same time, we recognize that Bob and Marilyn have been together for more than fifty years, and it's not likely they will change their patterns overnight. There will always be regrettable instances of criticism or insult, followed by blistering comebacks, and more hurt feelings. But if they make a commitment to switch to a more positive mode as often as they can, it will make a difference, John promises.

"Think about it like baseball," John suggests. "If a batter has a .300 average, he's having a terrific season—even though he's missing seventy percent of the balls! Communication in marriage can be like that—lots of missed opportunities, lots of failed attempts. But if do your best and your spouse knows you're trying, batting .300 can work out just fine."

One Year Later

The following year presented lots of challenges for Bob and Marilyn. Two of Marilyn's siblings passed away, and so did one of Bob's brothers.

"When you're dealing with your grief, you sometimes get tense and short with each other, so it's kind of hard," says Marilyn. And yet she notices that they have been sharing more thoughts and feelings with each other than they did in the past.

"We also seem to be listening to each other better," Bob adds.

Bob says he appreciates how they can now talk about their needs in ways that are safe and nonthreatening. "You don't have to build a wall around yourself and leave all these problems unresolved," he explains.

True to our prediction, the couple says they still slip into their old habit of criticize-and-defend. But now, at least, they can see a way out of those hurtful arguments. And, even more important, they understand there are ways to prevent them from occurring in the first place.

"This is not something you can say you've taken care of once and for all," says Marilyn. "You've got to be aware of it all the time. It's an everyday thing."

THE ANTIDOTES TO CONTEMPT: FONDNESS AND ADMIRATION

The kind of criticism and contempt that Bob and Marilyn demonstrated in their first lab conversation is typically a bad omen for marriages. And yet, when we ask them how they met and fell in love, we see something that gives us hope. Marilyn's eyes still shine as she describes the young soldier who proposed to her as "wonderful." And Bob still gazes proudly at his wife when he remembers her as "very attractive, very jolly, and very talkative." Despite all the arguments and bad feelings that have accumulated in recent years, the two still hold an ember of warm feelings for each other, especially when they remember how they first fell in love.

One key to a happier marriage is to keep fanning such sparks of good feeling about your partner, and here's why: Our research has shown that feelings of fondness and admiration are the perfect antidotes to contempt. When couples make a full, conscious effort to notice things they like about each other's personalities and character, and to express that fondness right out loud, their relationships typically improve.

So be on the lookout. Constantly scan your environment and observe your interactions. Rather than finding fault, look for evidence that your partner is getting it right. Catch your partner doing something right. Then express appreciation. Find excuses to offer compliments and praise. Examples might be the way she's fixed her hair, or the fact that he cleaned the snow off your car windshield. Maybe she went out of her way to find your favorite brand of ice cream. Maybe he offered to watch your favorite TV show when you both know he would have rather watched the baseball game. Try to notice all the small things that each of you contributes to your life together, and when you see them, let your partner know you've noticed and that you're grateful.

Quiz: Is There More Room for Fondness and Admiration in Your Marriage?

To assess the current state of fondness and admiration in your marriage, read the following statements and answer each "true" or "false."

PARTNER A   **PARTNER B**

T/F   T/F

____   1. I can easily list three things I most admire about my partner. ____

____   2. When we are apart, I think fondly of my partner.   ____

____   3. I often find some way to tell my partner "I love you."   ____

____   4. I often touch or kiss my partner affectionately.   ____

____   5. My partner really respects me.   ____

____   6. I feel loved and cared for in this relationship.   ____

____   7. I feel accepted and liked by my partner.   ____

____   8. My partner finds me sexy and attractive.   ____

____   9. My partner turns me on sexually.   ____

____   10. There is fire and passion in this relationship.   ____

____   11. Romance is definitely still part of our relationship.   ____

____   12. I am really proud of my partner.   ____

____   13. My partner really enjoys my achievements and
              accomplishments.   ____

____   14. I can easily tell you why I married my partner.   ____

____   15. If I had it all to do over again, I would marry the same
              person.   ____

____   16. We rarely go to sleep without some show of love or
              affection.   ____

____   17. When I come into a room, my partner is glad to see me.   ____

____   18. My partner appreciates the things I do in this marriage.   ____

____   19. My spouse generally likes my personality.   ____

____   20. Our sex life is generally satisfying.   ____

TO SCORE: Give yourself one point for each true (T) answer.

IF YOU SCORE 10 OR ABOVE: This is an area of strength for you. Your feelings of fondness and admiration will protect your marriage from the bad feelings that may come up between you.

IF YOU SCORE BELOW 10: Your marriage needs improvement in this area. You may need to take steps to revive positive feelings that were more obvious to you when your relationship began, or to build new feelings of fondness and admiration.

Exercise: Three Things I Like About You

Each of you chooses three characteristics from the list below that describe your partner. (If you see more than three, save the others to repeat the exercise another time.)

Loving	Funny	Vulnerable	Lusty
Sensitive	Considerate	Committed	Witty
Brave	Affectionate	Involved	Relaxed
Intelligent	Organized	Expressive	Beautiful
Thoughtful	Resourceful	Active	Handsome
Generous	Athletic	Careful	Rich
Loyal	Cheerful	Reserved	Calm
Truthful	Coordinated	Adventurous	Lively
Strong	Graceful	Receptive	A great partner
Energetic	Elegant	Reliable	A great parent
Sexy	Gracious	Responsible	Assertive
Decisive	Playful	Dependable	Protective
Creative	Caring	Nurturing	Sweet
Imaginative	A great friend	Warm	Tender
Fun	Exciting	Virile	Powerful
Attractive	Thrifty	Kind	Flexible
Interesting	Full of plans	Gentle	Understanding
Supportive	Shy	Practical	Totally silly

For each item you choose, think about an incident when your partner displayed this characteristic and it pleased you. Jot down some notes about this incident. Take turns sharing the traits and incidents with each other. Describe why this characteristic in him or her pleases you so much.

1. CHARACTERISTIC:_____

    INCIDENT:

2. CHARACTERISTIC:_____

    INCIDENT:

3. CHARACTERISTIC:_____

    INCIDENT:

Exercise: Nurturing Fondness in Your Relationship—A Seven-Week Plan

Have you ever had a gripe or an angry thought about your partner that you just couldn't release? Perhaps you had an argument and afterward you just kept playing that same negative thought over and over again in your mind. Or maybe you were feeling sad or angry for some other reason, but negative thoughts about your relationship kept coming up as well.

Our research shows that continually replaying negative thoughts about your partner can contribute to a downward spiral of distance and isolation in a marriage.

One solution is to train your mind to replace what we call "distress-maintaining" thoughts about your partner with "relationship-enhancing" thoughts. Doing so takes time and practice, but it's worth it because it can build feelings of fondness and admiration in your marriage.

Here's a seven-week plan for making this change. The plan provides five positive thoughts per week, and suggests an extra step or activity to make this thought stick. Many of these steps involve writing a few notes or journal entries, so you may want to keep a separate notebook or blank book for this purpose. If you don't like to write, just spend some time thinking about these topics and visualizing your ideas.

Think	Do
WEEK 1	
1. I genuinely like my partner.	List the one characteristic you find most endearing and lovable. Write about the time your partner showed this side best.
2. I can easily remember the joyful times in our marriage.	Pick one joyful time and write a short description of it.
3. I can easily remember romantic times in our marriage.	Pick one such time and describe the details about that time. Do you remember the setting, the mood, the feelings you had?
4. I am physically attracted to my partner.	Think of a physical attribute that pleases you. Spend some time fantasizing about this aspect of your partner.

Think	Do
5. My partner has specific qualities that make me feel proud.	Write down at least one characteristic. Under what circumstances do you usually feel this way?

WEEK 2

Think	Do
1. I feel a genuine sense of "we" rather than just "I" in this marriage.	Think of one thing that you have in common with your partner. Write about it or start a conversation with your partner about that issue.
2. We have some of the same general beliefs and values.	Describe one belief or value that you share. Think about how it feels to know that you and your partner provide a united front.
3. My spouse is my best friend.	What secrets have you and your spouse shared?
4. I can easily recall the time my spouse and I first met.	Write down the details you remember about your first romantic encounter with your spouse.
5. I get lots of support in this marriage.	Think of a time when you felt your spouse was really there for you.

continued

Think	Do
WEEK 3	
1. Our home is a place where I feel relaxed and not stressed.	Think about an instance when your spouse helped you to relax after a stressful time.
2. We have common goals.	List two such goals. Think about how it will feel to achieve them together.
3. I remember many details about deciding to get married.	Describe them in a paragraph.
4. There are some things about my partner that I don't like, but I can live with them.	List one of your spouse's minor faults that you feel you have learned to tolerate.
5. We share responsibilities for our life together.	Consider the way that you divide up chores on a regular basis.
WEEK 4	
1. We have a sense of control over our lives together.	Think of something important that you planned together that worked out well.
2. I am proud of this marriage.	Describe the aspect of your marriage that you're most proud of.
3. I am proud of my family.	Describe a specific time when you experienced this feeling.

Think	Do
4. I can recall happy memories about our wedding and honeymoon.	Describe at least one thing about these events that you enjoyed.
5. This marriage is a lot better than most I've seen.	Think of a marriage you know that's awful. Think about the way you've gotten past problems like these.

WEEK 5

Think	Do
1. I was really lucky to meet my spouse.	Write one benefit of being married to your spouse.
2. Marriage is sometimes a struggle, but it's worth it.	Write about a difficult incident or period of your lives that you weathered together.
3. There is a lot of affection between us.	Plan a surprise for your mate for tonight.
4. We are genuinely interested in each other.	Think of something to do or talk to your spouse about that you both find really interesting. Have that conversation.
5. We find each other to be good companions.	Plan an outing or trip together.

continued

Think	*Do*
WEEK 6	
1. My spouse is my confidant.	Think of times your spouse really listened and then gave you helpful advice.
2. My partner is an interesting person.	Think of a topic that interests both you and your spouse. Bring it up the next time you can just talk.
3. We respond well to each other.	Write a love letter to your spouse and mail it.
4. If I had it to do over again, I would marry the same person.	Plan a romantic getaway for your anniversary or other upcoming occasion.
5. There is lots of mutual respect in our marriage.	Plan to take a class together (sailing, cooking, ballroom dancing, etc.).
WEEK 7	
1. Sex is usually quite satisfying in this marriage.	Plan a romantic evening alone together.
2. We have come a long way together.	Make a list of all you have accomplished as a team.
3. I think we can weather any storm together.	Reminisce about having made it through a hard time.

Think	Do
4. We enjoy each other's sense of humor.	Rent a comedy film. Watch it together.
5. My mate can be very cute.	Get dressed up for an evening out.

"You Don't Care About My Dreams"

When architects Steve and Denise first met, they were thrilled to discover they shared so many interests—a love of nature, hiking, and travel. Coworkers at the same firm, they even liked the same books—especially those that inspire people to pursue their passions. Add to this mix a mutual attraction: Steve distinctly remembers first noticing "the freckles under Denise's eyes," and Denise was impressed by the way Steve's smile "could light up a room."

"This is going to be my first *real* relationship," thought Denise, who had recently left an unhappy marriage. For Steve, "being in a relationship with Denise seemed effortless."

But as even the most devoted couples learn, marriage can require lots of effort—especially when life tosses obstacles in the way of your dreams. That's certainly how it felt for Steve and Denise when, after a year of marriage, they learned they might not be able to have children.

Years of expensive fertility treatments, along with a series of miscarriages, put a serious strain on their marriage. Grief counseling and marital therapy taught them a great deal about communicating their feelings and supporting each other through difficult times. And eventually they conceived a baby whom Denise carried to term.

Logan was two years old when Steve and Denise visited our lab. And Denise, now a stay-at-home mom, was four months pregnant with their second child.

Despite their trials in eight years of marriage, Steve, thirty-eight, has remained an idealist who's not afraid to say what he wants—and doesn't want—from life. He loves backcountry adventure, playing the piano, and volunteering in his community, and he would like to have more time for these things in his life. But lately he feels trapped by the never-ending demands of his job and family life.

Steve's restlessness disturbs Denise, thirty-four, whose mom was recently diagnosed with a serious illness. Denise sometimes feels overwhelmed by the day-to-day responsibilities of caring for her mom and Logan, and she's worried that she may lose her current pregnancy. She says she wants to know that Steve is there for her, physically and emotionally. But these days she's not quite sure. This tension has led to some serious arguments, and that has them both concerned.

"Our fights come out of nowhere, with lots of passion behind them," says Steve. "It's especially bad when we're feeling stressed—like when we're paying the bills or when we were waiting for the results of a pregnancy test."

What's the Problem?

- *Steve and Denise don't address the dreams within their conflict—his dream of a more balanced life, her yearning for more security and support in times of crisis.*

- *Steve's failure to address her needs upsets Denise.*

- *Flooded with emotion, Denise can't hear and respond to Steve's attempts to take responsibility.*

- *Conversations get stalled.*

What's the Solution?

- *Postpone problem solving.*

- *Take turns talking about the dreams within the conflict.*

- *Look for areas of flexibility.*

- *Find ways to support the spirit of each other's dreams.*

Denise agrees. "Our arguments can be pretty explosive," she says.

To learn more about their conflicts, we ask them to rehash a recent disagreement. Denise recalls the day she unexpectedly had to take her mom to the doctor. Meanwhile, she wanted Steve to pick up Logan at the babysitter's house. But Steve had other plans. He was supposed to volunteer for a cancer support group that afternoon, caring for a child whose brother was getting chemotherapy.

What They Say	What We Notice
Denise: I was actually kind of angry with you. I felt frustrated because you were helping this family in crisis. But your own wife is going through a crisis, too—hoping to hold on to this pregnancy, helping my mom, and we've got our own son to take care of.	+ Expresses her frustration. − Attempts to make Steve feel guilty. − Doesn't say what she needs.
Steve: I think everything you're saying is legitimate in the short term. My concern is our long-term goals. We've talked about our ideals—things like volunteering and playing piano and having time to play with Logan. And volunteering is a real big part of it. If I give up volunteering, it just sends me into this funk of "All I do is work." I realize that the day-to-day demands have snared me. I have these passions and I just get slapped down every time.	+/− Starts by validating her, but doesn't really respond to her complaint. + Expresses his needs. − Blaming. − Criticizes her.

What They Say	What We Notice
Denise: When you say "the day-to-day snares," I wonder, am *I* a day-to-day snare? That's number one. And number two is, you could have let this little boy's mother know that you might not be there. I mean, the weekend I found out my mom was sick again, I was supposed to be doing my volunteer work. But I just immediately called the person and canceled. I said, "I'm sorry, I can't deal with this. My mom is seriously ill." So I'm really frustrated. I know about your dreams, and I know it's really been hard for both of us to makes our dreams meet. But where am *I* in this? Am I hindering you from your dreams? Or am I part of them?	+ Expresses her fear. − Blaming, one-upping him. + Expresses her insecurity, her needs.
Steve: I agree. We could sit down and decide, does my volunteering fit in? And we could really talk about that.	+ Responds without becoming defensive. − Doesn't respond to her need for reassurance.
Denise: But throughout life, these kinds of things are going to come up. You're not going have enough time to . . .	− Ignores his response.
Steve *(interrupting)*: I think . . . I'm sorry, go ahead.	+ Stops himself from interrupting.
Denise: No, I'm sorry, you go ahead.	+ Shows willingness to listen to him.

continued

What They Say	What We Notice
Steve: I think we need to bring a little closure to this, and maybe I have some thoughts you might want to hear.	− Tries to close the conversation before hearing her out.
Denise: Yeah, we need to keep the conversation more to the issue of volunteering.	+/− Shows willingness to work with him, but she gives up trying to be heard.
Steve: I think, long-term, we need to ask, "Do these volunteer opportunities work?" But as far as the immediate need, I probably wasn't clear with you. I didn't tell you that I was prepared to pick Logan up that afternoon. My problem is I didn't communicate that.	+ Takes responsibility for the problem.
Denise: Yeah, I agree. Because inside, I was thinking, this is *my mom*! And I realize that this other family is in a crisis, but this is like, you know . . .	+/− Expresses more feelings, but slips into blaming again.
Steve: I wasn't picking up the slack with Logan.	+ Validates her feelings. + Takes responsibility.
Denise: I think I was so emotional, and it was just so hard for me to say, "I just don't feel OK with what you're doing."	+ Takes responsibility. + Expresses insight into her own feelings.

What They Say	What We Notice
Steve: I think when these things happen, we need to come together and identify the problem. Say, "Steve, there's going to be a problem in how we deal with Logan at dinnertime. I don't have an answer for that problem and then the two of us need to sit down."	– Moving into problem solving before they've explored all their feelings. – Puts the responsibility on her.
Denise: I agree. But what gets me anxious is I know your mind doesn't work the same way my mind does, so I'm afraid that there won't be enough time . . .	+ Expresses her fear.
Steve *(interrupting)*: There is nothing wrong with you saying, "Steve, there's a problem here." I'm not going to say, "I'll get back to you in three days." Once again, the problem is I was perfectly willing to deal with Logan, and I just never mentioned it.	– Interrupts her. – Tries again to put most of the responsibility on her. – Defensive.
Denise: I can't read your mind.	– Defensive. – Slightly blaming.
Steve: Right. I need to verbalize what my intentions are. I'm just not very good about bringing them out.	+ Takes responsibility. – Trying again to close the issue before they've really expressed their feelings.

continued

129

What They Say	What We Notice
Denise: For me, it's more than that. I feel like your volunteering is just creeping in to take more and more of your time. It's creating more resentment, and I just feel over-whelmed by that. Because I am trying to keep everything else going.	+ Keeps trying to express her feel-ings, even though the process isn't working.

Our Analysis: Ignoring Dreams Beneath the Conflict Stalls Communication

Unlike the "explosive" arguments they describe having at home, Steve and Denise have done a good job of avoiding hostility in this discussion. They're talking about some very difficult issues, and yet their tone remains civil. They don't attack each other, and they express surprisingly little defensiveness. That's a real plus.

But they're not making much progress. Much like Mike and Maria in chapter 3, Steve is so focused on solving their immediate problem (his volunteer schedule) that they miss the chance to talk about issues beneath the conflict. That is, Denise needs Steve's reassurance that she has his support—especially during hard times like this one. And Steve wants to know that Denise respects his dream that he can still have a life of joy and adventure, even with their mounting responsibilities. Although both partners are expressing their own needs in this conversation, they are not doing a very good job of responding to each other.

Upset that her feelings are ignored, Denise becomes flooded with emotion. The trouble peaks when Denise hears Steve refer to their life together as a "snare." In the seconds following that remark, the heart monitor Denise is wearing indicates that her heart rate jumps from 95 beats per minute to 115.

"Any heart rate above 100 is going to interfere with your ability to focus and to concentrate," John explains. Consequently, Denise doesn't respond to Steve's attempts to take responsibility for the problem. In fact, Steve tries three times to tell Denise that he made a mistake that day by not conveying that he planned to pick up Logan. But Denise never acknowledges these attempts to repair the relationship. She's so frustrated by his failure to respond to her feelings that she can't get on board with his efforts to move on.

As the conversation continues to go nowhere fast, it's easy to see how tension could build and tempers might flare—especially if they were having this conversation at home amid the stress of caring for their toddler or rushing to doctors' appointments.

Our Advice

"It's important to recognize and honor the dreams and feelings within your conflict," John tells Steve and Denise. Couples may try to brush aside such issues in order to deal with the crisis of the day, but that doesn't make the conflict go away. And until dreams and feelings are recognized and honored, the conflict is going to keep resurfacing in ways that are often frustrating and sometimes painful.

What is the best way to uncover hidden dreams? By taking a step back from conflict, and exploring each person's position on a deeper level. The conversation can include questions like "Why is this issue so important to you?" and "Is there some story behind this that I should understand? Is it related to something important from your past?" (See the exercise "Responding to the Dreams Within Your Conflict" on page 145 for more questions.)

Once both partners get a chance to express their dreams and each feels understood, then they look for areas of flexibility and compromise. The idea is for each partner to come away from the conversation feeling as if his or her dream was respected and honored in some way.

It's not the kind of conversation you can have on the run. That's why it's so important for couples to have time alone together on a weekly basis at least—time to talk uninterrupted for an hour or two about what's happening in their lives, time to share their thoughts, feelings, and dreams about their life together.

We suggest that Steve and Denise try an exercise we developed for just this kind of conversation. The topic will be the same as last time—their conflict over his volunteer schedule. But this time we encourage them to try to uncover their individual dreams within that conflict.

As with many of our exercises, we suggest that Steve and Denise take turns as the speaker and listener. When one is talking, the other simply tries to draw that person out. Neither person should try to defend what they did that day. Nor should they try to debate the issues or persuade one another.

"Think of this as a fact-finding mission," says John, "not a problem-solving session." And yet, once partners try this exercise and start talking about the meaning beneath their conflicts, they may find it much easier to solve near-term problems in the future. "Sometimes when couples do this exercise, we literally see their fists open up," says John. "And once they relax, their dreams emerge, leading to better understanding and compromise."

What They Say	What We Notice
Steve: What part of my volunteering has really created the most concern for you?	+ Asking about her feelings is a great way to start.
Denise: It seemed like you were more wrapped up in how this other family was coping with their crisis than what was happening in our own home—the challenges we were facing with my pregnancy and my mom.	+/− Starting to express her needs, but still doing it in a blaming way.

What They Say	What We Notice
Steve: So it sounds like you were sensitive to how I was prioritizing things in our family below my volunteering.	+ Reflects back her feelings.
Denise: Yeah. I had a sense that our family would accommodate whatever other obligations you have in your life. Telling that other family, "I'm sorry, I can't do it," didn't seem like an option for you. And yet it is an option for you to tell me or Logan that. Sometimes I wonder, is it ever flipped? Does your family ever become the obligation that *always* gets met?	+/− Trying to express her own needs, but still too focused on blaming Steve.
Steve: How does it make you feel when I prioritize the family that way?	+ Great nondefensive response.
Denise: I certainly understand that it's easier to do this to the people you're closest to. Because you know we love you and we try to be there for each other. But I also wonder, what if I really needed it to be different? Most of the time I can really handle things, but when I get into these emotional crises, I panic.	+ Expresses understanding for Steve's position. + Expresses love for him. + Finally says what she needs.
Steve: Was it just this instance, or are you worried about what might happen in a future, more serious time?	+ Good question to explore her feelings.

continued

What They Say	What We Notice
Denise: Well, I'm not worried about you leaving the relationship. I just wonder whether I'm lumped into all of the things you have to fend off. You spoke of your dreams. Well, what about the day-to-day living with me, just the ordinary stuff that we have to do? Is our life together as important to you as your dreams of traveling, or kayaking more, or volunteering more? Or am I really just one of those things that has to happen? Because I like to be at the top of your priorities, but sometimes I'm not sure.	+ Good, honest questions. + Reveals her feelings of insecurity and her need for reassurance.
Steve: So it sounds like you're scared that I associate you with the mundane obligations of life. Are there ways that I can help you understand that you are part of my passion? That being with you is part of my dream?	+ Shows he's really listening. + Strong reassurance. + Asks her what she needs.
Denise: Well, we've talked about the idea of really making time for each other. I like the way you always take Logan on Friday afternoons. And I know this really isn't about me, but it's a really neat feeling to know that I can look in your calendar and there it is. From twelve to five o'clock on Friday, you're going to be with Logan.	+ Now that she feels reassured, she can begin to move into problem solving. + Tells him what she wants and needs. + Expresses appreciation for him.
Steve: OK. I'll try to think of more ways I can do that for you, too.	+ Acknowledges her needs. + Takes responsibility.

What They Say	What We Notice

(Time is up, so they switch sides. Steve starts by talking about the way volunteering fits into his dreams of how he'd like his life to be.)

Steve: I'm the guy who always wonders why we have to work so hard, or why there is so much pain and anger in life. That's why I use that term "the daily grind." I know the joy I've felt when I've been on a hike with you and we're standing up on the side of the mountain. Or when we're in the kayak, or I'm playing some tunes on the piano. That joy is just so profound that I wonder, why can't I always experience that? My volunteering is a part of that. And it's a very impractical, very ideal way of looking at it. But when I see threats to my volunteering, it feels like I'm missing out, and that feels like a big loss.	+ Expresses his dreams, his desires. + Reassures her by including her in his dream.
Denise: If one of those items isn't there, do you somehow feel that you've been cheated?	+ Good questions; nondefensive.

continued

What They Say	What We Notice
Steve: I just have this sense that I've let things get out of balance. When was the last time we were in the mountains together? I think that I've neglected that part of my life for so long that I react to any little thing you ask for as "Wow, one more person that needs something." That's why I want to talk more about the way I've been equating you with the person that needs things versus what I want in my dreams. It really works both ways. I want you to be part of my dreams. I'd rather have you on a train with me in India or in a kayak on the Sound than sitting at home making sure there are no stains on the kitchen floor. When I'm talking about that train in India, I forget to tell you, "You're by my side. And if you're not, I don't want to be on that train." I just haven't been clear about that. I want to take you and Logan away. I want to go to India. I want to play piano and have all three of us downstairs playing drums and piano and dancing. I just want all three of us to be joyful. But it's amazing how the mortgage just keeps coming in every month.	+ Honestly expressing his needs. + Expresses insight about his feelings. + Expresses his desire to be close to her and to have her be part of his dream. + Reassures her that he wants to be with her. + Expresses his frustration with day-to-day demands.
Denise: I'm just wondering, if diapers have to be changed, and bills have to be paid, and floors have to be scrubbed, do you wish that all these mundane things would just go away?	+ Expressing her worries. + Asking about his thoughts and feelings.

What They Say	What We Notice
Steve: I just get this sense that I've neglected my dreams for so long that I'm saturated with the mundane things. I think if we just got a dose of regular walks in Magnuson Park, or a short trip to Mexico now and then, things would be better. I could bring myself back to center where washing dishes is no big deal.	+ Expresses his feelings. + Takes responsibility for those feelings. + Expresses willingness to compromise.
Denise: Right.	+ Communicates understanding.
Steve: It's not that washing the dishes is so bad. It's just I can't remember the last time I was on a train. Just a train ride to Portland! I've just neglected that for too long.	+ Expresses his feelings.

At the end of this conversation, we're impressed by the affection and interest Steve and Denise have displayed. It's great that Steve was willing to express his dreams *and* listen to Denise's feelings.

Steve says he found the talk "freeing" because he didn't feel obligated to find the perfect solution right at that moment. "I didn't feel like I had to make it go somewhere, so I was able to build my thoughts as I went along," he explains. "I could say, 'Maybe this is what's going on inside.'"

Both partners are more responsive and more open to each other's influence this time. This allows them to take the conversation in a positive direction instead of a negative one.

Still, Denise feels a bit worried. She hears Steve's affection for her, but she's going to need lots of reassurance that he's not staying in the relationship because he feels trapped; he's there because he wants to be. "I'm still afraid I'll keep him from those dreams and he'll reach a point where he goes, 'This just isn't good for me,' " she says. "We have trouble even finding time for little walks in Magnuson Park."

It's true. With a two-year-old and an infant, packing an afternoon picnic can feel like a major troop movement. But we remind them that this is just a stage their family is going through while their children are small. During this time, it's important to honor the *spirit* of each other's dreams—even if you're not in the position to make those dreams come true right now.

"If adventure is something that you both value, then perhaps it's something that you do in little pieces today—while continuing to dream of big adventures later on," says Julie. "Kayaking in Puget Sound may not be a trip to India, but both adventures have that same dreamlike quality for Steve. And he wants to share that with you, Denise. He's not about to give that up."

Steve's suggestion of a train trip to Portland is a great idea. It keeps his dreams of travel alive while they're dealing with diapers and nap schedules. And if Steve can show Denise—with his actions as well as his words—that he's there to share the responsibilities of raising the kids and caring for her mom, she'll be reassured that he's honoring her feelings as well.

Another key is to take the time needed to fully explore the dreams within the conflict. "You may not be able to do it the very moment a conflict happens—especially if your heart rate is 115 beats a minute," John reminds them. "When that's happening, you may be too flooded to think and to communicate clearly." So take a "time out" and promise to revisit the issue when you can talk calmly about it without interruption, he advises. The exercise on page 62 ("Calm Down to Avoid Flooding") may be useful. And the exercises at the end of this chapter can help you explore the dreams within your conflicts.

One Year Later

It's been a great year for Steve and Denise. Their new baby boy arrived on time, healthy and strong. Denise's mom recovered from her illness. And they bought a new home near the beaches of Puget Sound. They purposely chose a house with a big garage so they could keep the kayaks handy for spontaneous day trips.

Both Steve and Denise have quit their volunteer jobs—although Denise says she'd like to do more when the boys are older. "It may be something like distributing groceries for a food bank—something that Logan could get involved in."

The idea of taking the boys along is catching on. At age three, Logan has already been kayaking, snowshoeing, and hiking in the mountains. "We're not going off to India for a while, but I can see that we'll be doing a lot of wandering with the boys," says Steve.

The couple is also making a conscious effort to improve communication around day-to-day family needs. They now set aside time each Sunday night to discuss their schedule for the week ahead—a ritual Denise finds reassuring. "It helps us to see things down the pike that might create turmoil. Like if I have a doctor's appointment that's going to throw dinner off schedule, Steve might say, 'How can I help? What can I do to make things easier?'"

Denise says she still feels harried sometimes, which can lead to worries about her marriage. "But then the kids will go over to Mom's so Steve and I can get some time alone together. And I'm always amazed at how immediately we're able to connect again."

Your Hidden Dreams and Aspirations: The "Prairie Dogs" of Marital Conflict

Our research shows that all marriages experience a certain number of perpetual conflicts—differences that don't go away, no matter what. Conflicts may differ from couple to couple; while one pair may constantly disagree over money and housework, another may continually clash over religion and parenting.

Since perpetual conflicts don't disappear, the goal is to live with them in ways that allow understanding, dialogue, and compromise. Failure to do so can lead to gridlocked conflict—a condition where partners are so entrenched in their own positions that there's no give-and-take. Putting up with gridlocked conflict is a bad idea because it leads to the kind of frustration, resentment, and anger that can be very harmful to a marriage.

So how do you avoid—or break out of—such gridlock? One of the best ways is to explore the dreams within your disagreements. By dreams, we mean the individual hopes and aspirations within each position on the issue that each person has—the dreams that are attached to your life history and that hold a lot of meaning in your life. Those dreams may be linked to your sense of identity—for example, what it means to be a member of your family, your race, or your religion. They may be connected to deep philosophical beliefs you hold about issues like power or love or loyalty. When you talk about those dreams, you may say things like, "That's just the way I am," or "I've always felt this way."

The trouble is, the connection between a couple's gridlocked conflict and their dreams is not always apparent. That's because we hold our dreams so close to our hearts that talking about them can make us feel quite vulnerable. In fact, we have referred to dreams as "the prairie dogs of marital conflict." Prairie dogs are elusive little creatures that live in complex tunnels beneath the surface of the earth, only popping up when they can be sure there are no predators about to attack. If they sense an enemy in their midst, they're gone in a flash. In the same way, our dreams only come to the surface of our interactions when we feel that it's safe to share them. Otherwise, the only thing our partners see is our position in the conflict.

Just because a dream is hidden, however, doesn't mean it's not driving the conversation. Here's a common example: A couple with a joint checking account discovers that one partner has failed to track all expenditures. The argument that results is about more than writing down numbers in a checkbook. It has to do with each partner's closely held dreams about issues of power, loyalty, honesty, security, freedom, and so on.

Partners may have a hard time revealing and hearing each other's deepest feelings about these dreams as long as they're arguing about the checkbook, however. To make the environment secure enough for dreams to emerge, you have to stop debating the issue and start creating an environment that's safe enough for dreams within each position to emerge. Once you get all your dreams out on the table, you may see each other's positions from a surprising new perspective. You may even find yourself saying things like "I had no idea this was so important to you. No wonder you couldn't yield on that. Now I understand why you've had to stand your ground." And as a consequence, you may be in a better position to start talking about areas of flexibility and compromise. The following exercises will give you some guidance for doing just that. Help is also available at the end of chapter 10, in the section called "Don't Get Gridlocked over Perpetual Issues."

Quiz: What Are the Dreams Within Your Conflicts?

With your partner, scan the list of dreams on the next page. In the second column, indicate which partner feels strongly about that dream. Now think about a recent disagreement. Can you see how this dream might be related to that disagreement? If so, have the partner who feels strongly about that dream jot down some notes about that conflict. Then share the exercise on page 145, which may help you discuss the dreams beneath your conflict and find some common ground.

Dream	This dream is important to:	How the dream relates to your conflict
Examples:		
A sense of freedom	<u>Jack</u>	Our summer vacation (I really want to run away with you to Hawaii instead of going to Nebraska.)
Knowing my family	<u>Jill</u>	Our summer vacation (Having you beside me at my family reunion in Nebraska means so much to me.)
A sense of freedom	____	
The experience of peace	____	
Unity with nature	____	
Exploring who I am	____	
Adventure	____	
A spiritual journey	____	
Justice	____	
Honor	____	
Unity with my past	____	
Healing	____	
Knowing my family	____	

Dream	This dream is important to:	How the dream relates to your conflict
Becoming all I can be	____	
Having a sense of power	____	
Dealing with my aging	____	
Exploring a creative side of myself	____	
Becoming more powerful	____	
Getting over past hurts	____	
Becoming more competent	____	
Asking God for forgiveness	____	
Exploring an old part of myself I have lost	____	
Getting over a personal hangup	____	
Having a sense of order	____	
Being able to be productive	____	
A place and a time to just "be"	____	
Being able to truly relax	____	

143

Dream	This dream is important to:	How the dream relates to your conflict
Reflecting on my life	_____	
Getting my priorities in order	_____	
Finishing something important	_____	
Exploring the physical side of myself	_____	
Being able to compete and win	_____	
Travel	_____	
Quiet	_____	
Atonement	_____	
Building something important	_____	
Ending a chapter of my life	_____	
Saying good-bye to something	_____	
Finding love	_____	
Other:_____	_____	
Other:_____	_____	

Exercise: Responding to the Dreams Within Your Conflict

1. When a conflict comes up, use the chart on pages 142–144 to identify the dreams that each of you has within that conflict.

2. Designate one person as the speaker and the other as the listener.

3. The speaker tells the listener all about his or her dream. The listener's job is to draw the information out of the speaker using questions like these:

- What's important to you about this dream?

- What's the most important part?

- Why is this part important?

- Is there a story behind this for you? Tell me that story.

- Is there something from your life history that relates to that story?

- Tell me all the feelings that you have about this dream.

- Are there any feelings you left out? What do you wish for here?

- What would be your ideal dream here?

- How do you imagine things would be if you got what you wanted?

- Is there a deeper purpose or goal in this for you?

- Does this relate to some belief or value for you?

- Do you have some fear about not having this dream honored? Do you imagine some disaster?

The listener should not try to debate the issue or express opinions about the speaker's dream. In fact, neither partner should use this exercise to try to convince the other that his or her position in the conflict is the "right" position.

145

4. When the speaker is done, switch roles and explore the other partner's dreams.

5. Once your dreams are out in the open, look for ways that *each partner* can be flexible in order to honor the other partner's dreams.

6. If you find it hard to support your partner's dream, try this:

- Visualize your partner's dream as two concentric circles.

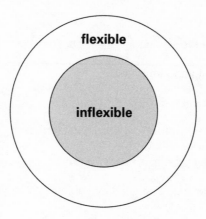

- The "inflexible" middle circle holds the part of your dream that you must have honored. (Example: Steve needs some sense of adventure, even if his dream of traveling to India can't be honored right now, when they have small children.)

- The outside "flexible" circle holds the part of your own dream that you *can* be flexible about. (Example: Denise can support the spirit of Steve's dreams by going along with smaller adventures for now—i.e., by kayaking close to home and by daydreaming with him of bigger adventures once the kids are older.) Try to make that outer circle as big as possible by searching for common ground and honoring your partner's dream.

- If you're having trouble filling the outside circle, consider the various levels of support you might offer and ask, how far am I willing to go? Examples:

  LEVEL 1. I can respect your dream.

  LEVEL 2. I can respect your dream and agree to learn more about it.

  LEVEL 3. I can financially support your dream to some degree.

  LEVEL 4. I can join you in your dream to some degree.

  LEVEL 5. I'm on board. Let's go for it.

- Realize that this is an issue of compromise, and compromise never feels perfect. Each person has to be willing to give something away in order to receive something in return. The important thing is that each person feels his or her dreams are understood, respected, and honored.

CHAPTER 6

"You're So Distant and Irritable All the Time"

Kevin was new to Boston and working part-time as a janitor the first time he met Suzanne. He remembers her sassy haircut, the flannel shirt she wore, and the casual chat they shared as he cleaned her office. Her "sparkly smile" made such an impression that when he spotted her two years later, he made the connection.

"I was at this friend's art opening and he walked into the gallery and said, 'Suzanne! Suzanne! It's me, Kevin!' And I was like, 'Hi! Who are you?'" Suzanne tells us, laughing. "But I thought he was a nice guy!"

Two years later still, they met again at that same friend's holiday party. This time it was Kevin who made the impression. "He just radiated warmth," Suzanne says. "I remember looking in his eyes and feeling very drawn in, very comfortable. I was intrigued."

The next day, Suzanne sent him a box of chocolate-covered cherries with a note that read, "Kevin, I'm really enjoying getting to know you."

"I didn't open the box for twenty-four hours," says Kevin. "I just kept looking at it, saying, 'My goodness! My goodness!'"

Looking back, Suzanne believes it was Kevin's persistent friendliness and optimism that allowed their romance to take flight. And after seven years of marriage, they say they'd like to recapture the affection and passion they once shared. "When we do connect, it's just wonderful," says Suzanne, thirty-five. "There's so much humor and fun."

But these days that sense of connection eludes them. They're feeling isolated from each other emotionally and physically—and that distresses them both.

"It's like we're not a team anymore," says Kevin, forty-two.

"So what is it that's coming between you?" John asks.

"The bills," Kevin answers immediately, as though it were a reflex.

"I don't think it's that," adds Suzanne quietly.

"OK, so it's taking the dog out every morning and every night," Kevin says, using sarcasm to drive home his point. For him, even the simplest routines have become a source of irritation.

Childless by choice, Kevin and Suzanne make a decent living—he

What's the Problem?

- Kevin is depressed and withdraws.
- Both feel isolated, lonely.
- Suzanne gets critical and controlling in efforts to connect with Kevin.
- Kevin resists talking about his sadness.
- When Kevin finally talks about his feelings, Suzanne gets uncomfortable and sidetracks.

What's the Solution?

- Seek treatment for Kevin's depression.
- Be willing to listen to each other's feelings.
- Ask questions that encourage emotional sharing.
- Don't lose sight of Suzanne's needs.

as a paralegal and she as a speech therapist. Still, Kevin worries a lot about money. For years he's been trying to convince himself—and Suzanne—that if they could just make more and spend less, maybe he wouldn't feel so hopeless and tired all the time.

"When Kevin feels that he's not making enough money, he retreats," Suzanne explains. He stops talking, spends a lot of time alone, and becomes increasingly irritable.

Kevin explains that solitude makes him feel better in the short term. "But quickly things start to back up on me," he adds. "My productivity goes down. And I get angry—at the dog, the cats, and at Suzanne."

Suzanne has her own problems with productivity because of a rare blood disorder that causes occasional bouts of fatigue. When she's not feeling well, she'd like to rely on Kevin for comfort. But his moodiness makes that difficult. She admits that she sometimes reacts to Kevin's withdrawal by picking a fight. She criticizes the way he's driving or cooking, for example, because an argument feels less lonely than no connection at all. But in the end, it always backfires. Rather than drawing Kevin closer, poking at him makes him even more irritable, more withdrawn.

Although they can still connect, talk, and share deep feelings at times, these occasions are becoming less frequent. Meanwhile, both are feeling increasingly sad and lonely, and neither knows the way out of their predicament. After evaluating their questionnaires and hearing them talk about their interactions, however, we begin to suspect that Kevin's dark moods are one source of the problem.

"Can I be frank?" Julie asks, turning to Kevin. "I think you're depressed. And it's really crippling you in some way. It's causing you to withdraw, to shut down. It's making you feel like a failure."

It may also damage your marriage, Julie continues. "I can see, Suzanne, that you love this man so much, but you feel stumped. You try to reach out with affection and talking, but you don't get much back. So then you try to reach out with criticism, and that doesn't work, either. You're stymied."

Depression can be like a third party coming between partners and creating a sense of hopelessness, Julie adds. And unless the partners are willing to talk about it, improving the marriage may be impossible.

Kevin protests at first, pointing to the "stigma" of admitting he's depressed. But we assure him that the depression is not his fault. Often it's caused by a chemical imbalance that can be treated with counseling and medication.

We also emphasize that talking to Suzanne about the problem is essential to healing their relationship. If they can learn to connect with each other during the dark times, both partners will feel less isolated from each other. They'll view each other as allies in their efforts to battle Kevin's depression, to cope with Suzanne's illness, and to win back more loving feelings for each other.

Here's what happens when Kevin and Suzanne agree to talk about these issues:

What They Say	What We Notice
Kevin: You know, Suzanne, I *am* depressed. I'm sorry, because it puts this wall between us. It keeps me from moving on.	+ Good honest expression of feeling. + Acknowledges how it affects her.
Suzanne: Well, honey, do you think your dad was depressed?	+/− Shows interest, but backs away by shifting the attention to Kevin's father.
Kevin: Yeah, I think my father was depressed.	−/+ Responds.
Suzanne: What do you think that was about?	− Continues to sidetrack.
Kevin: About his history. *(He sighs and then falls silent.)*	− Appears discouraged, but he's not telling her why.

What They Say	What We Notice
Suzanne: You know, I think so many people feel that way. I feel that way a lot, too.	− Minimizes at first, as though it's "no big deal." + Supportive statement that she understands how he feels.
Kevin: I just feel like a fake.	+ More feeling.
Suzanne: How come?	+ Shows interest.
Kevin: Because I don't do anything. You know that I want to write. But it's like, "You want to write about life? You don't even want to live it."	+ More feeling.
Suzanne: You're being so hard on yourself! How come?	+/− Question shows she's listening, but "How come?" may lead them into intellectualizing rather than sharing feelings.
Kevin: I don't know. I feel kind of flat. There's definitely something missing in my life. And this past week has been really tough because I have been so tired. Fatigued.	+ Doesn't try to analyze; continues to share feelings.
Suzanne: Yeah, I worry about you.	+ Shares her own feelings; acknowledges that she cares.
Kevin: And I've already told you, I just feel old.	+ Reveals more.

What They Say	What We Notice
Suzanne: Oh, you! Honey, you know what I was thinking? We haven't really been exercising. You used to be so athletic. I think we should do something together. I really think we should look into the tandem bike. I know it's expensive, but . . .	− Minimizes; looking for a quick fix.
Kevin: There are a lot of tandems out there that don't get used.	− Resistant because it's too early for problem solving.
Suzanne: Well, yeah, but we can just rent one for a while.	− Ignores his resistance; keeps trying to problem solve.
Kevin: I feel like I'm depressed. There is now an eight-hundred-pound gorilla in the room.	+ States his feelings once more, this time telling her how big the problem is.
Suzanne: I'm totally—I'm acknowledging that. So tell me more about it. What does it feel like to be depressed? Do things feel dark and heavy?	+ Great response, asking him to describe how it feels.
Kevin: Heavy. Heavy. I look at my brother. And he seems to have so much energy.	+ Responds; shares feelings about himself in relation to his brother.
Suzanne: You think? What does your brother talk about when you call him?	− Backs away by asking him about his brother rather than his own feelings.

continued

What They Say	What We Notice
Kevin: Everything that's not him. I don't know. I have had a hard time doing anything. I make endless lists.	+ Gets the conversation back on track.
Suzanne: Do you feel like your work is challenging for you?	+/– Asking a question is great, but again it's analytical—taking him away from his feelings.
Kevin: It's challenging. But nothing I'm incapable of. I just don't think I have any passion for life right now.	+/– Subtly lets her know he doesn't want to go there, but he's not telling her what he needs from her—empathy. + Opens up further.
Suzanne: So really anything you'd do right now, you don't feel like you could be passionate about.	+ Reflecting back his feelings, shows she's listening.
Kevin: I just feel like I don't have any tools to do anything. I feel like I am dark and in that fetal position.	+ More feelings.
Suzanne: How long has this been going on?	+ Good question.
Kevin: Well, I would say since the Cuban Missile Crisis.	–/+ A bit sarcastic, but he really wants her to get how important this is.
Suzanne: Before I was born! Was there ever a time when you felt alive and not depressed?	+ She shows she gets it. +/– Question shows interest, but takes the focus off here and now.

What They Say	What We Notice
Kevin: Certainly when I first moved here. That was an incredibly alive time for me.	+ Responds.
Suzanne: How come?	+/− Again, good to ask questions, but still too analytical.
Kevin: It felt like I had taken ankle weights off. I was floating. I don't know. Now I feel like I'm in a perpetually overcast mood. But until I just got fingered, I could keep fooling myself. But now we both know and I can't.	+ Shares feelings. + Tells her what he needs: for both of them to face the issue.

Our Analysis: Avoiding Emotional Intensity Postpones Healing

When the conversation ends, Suzanne says she's relieved to understand finally why Kevin has been so distant. At the same time, Kevin tells us he's amazed that Suzanne isn't angry: "Why doesn't she say, 'You bastard! *You've* been the problem all this time!'?"

The reason, of course, is Suzanne's deep concern for Kevin, which she demonstrates in this conversation. In turn, she finally gets what she needs—some honest, open communication from him about his feelings. She also demonstrates her love with interested questions and compassionate responses, John observes. Still, we spot ways that these questions and responses could be even better. For instance, Suzanne has a tendency to avoid the intensity of Kevin's emotions by introducing side topics to the conversation. She brings up issues such as Kevin's dad's depression and Kevin's need for exercise. While these topics are related, talking about them in this moment takes Kevin away from sharing his feelings with her and therefore interferes with their process of building intimacy.

155

Suzanne also makes the common error of rushing into a problem-solving mode too early. Suggesting they purchase a tandem bike could be helpful later on, but as Kevin's reaction shows, he's not ready to start this kind of brainstorming yet. First, he needs Suzanne to spend more time listening to him express his feelings. He won't be ready to talk about solutions with her until he feels reassured that she can understand and accept what he's saying. We suspect Suzanne may not feel completely comfortable with the depth of emotion that Kevin is sharing. Perhaps she, too, is scared of the uncertain implications. But if she can learn to hang in there with him as he processes his feelings, she'll be helping to reestablish a connection that's been missing from their relationship and that may even help him to recover.

In addition, Suzanne's open-ended questions show sincere interest in Kevin's problems. She's doing her best to draw him out. The ways she's phrasing some of her questions could be a problem, however. Questions like "Why?" or "How come?" draw answers that come from the head instead of the heart. Kevin and Suzanne don't need the intellectual exercise of analyzing Kevin's problems right now. Rather, they need to share their feelings about those problems. Her question "What does it feel like to be depressed?" is more likely to draw a helpful response. We advise her to avoid "why" questions.

And, finally, we notice that Kevin and Suzanne never get around to discussing Suzanne's needs and feelings. That's not surprising, considering that Kevin's revelations about his depression are so new to them. Still, we want them to be aware that, even in a crisis, both partners' needs must be recognized and considered.

Our Advice

Kevin's willingness to talk about his depression, and Suzanne's willingness to listen, is a great sign that they can grow closer. To help this process along, we offer this advice:

1. BE A CARING WITNESS TO EACH OTHER'S STRONG, NEGATIVE FEELINGS

"It's hard for partners to believe that they're doing anything for each other when they're just sitting there, considering the other person's sadness or frustration," John explains. "But usually it's enough to just be present and to empathize. Think of yourselves as two birds sitting on the same perch, viewing the world, and chirping together. That sense of togetherness can be sufficient." In fact, trying to problem-solve too soon can interfere with intimacy. "Remember, your goal isn't to fix the feelings; it's to help each other feel less alone," John advises.

2. ASK QUESTIONS THAT LEAD TO THE HEART INSTEAD OF THE HEAD

Instead of asking "why" or "how come" questions—which lead to analysis—we encourage Suzanne and Kevin to ask each other questions that require them to consider their feelings. Examples: "How are you feeling about this right now?" or "What is the most difficult part of this experience for you?" (For more ideas, see the exercise called "Establish a Ritual for Stress-Reducing Conversation" on page 167.)

3. DON'T LOSE TRACK OF SUZANNE'S NEEDS

With so much focus on Kevin's depression, it would be easy for Suzanne to fall into the role of a caretaker who never expresses her own needs. This would not be good for either partner, or for their marriage. During our session, Kevin tells Suzanne that he feels most "involved" in their relationship *when she needs him* emotionally. So, in addition to talking about *his* internal world, the pair needs to make room in their conversations for Suzanne's concerns. What are her worries, her goals, her desires? What can Kevin do to offer her reassurance and comfort?

4. GET TREATMENT FOR DEPRESSION

We urge Kevin to talk to his doctor or a mental health professional about treatment for depression. This could include counseling, antidepressant medication, or both. We reiterate that depression is often caused by a biochemical imbalance, and that there's no shame in asking for help.

In this next dialogue we ask Kevin and Suzanne simply to continue their conversation about Kevin's depression, keeping our advice in mind.

What They Say	What We Notice
Kevin: On the one hand I'm thinking, geez, how much is this going to cost?	+ Expresses worry.
Suzanne: *(smiles and rolls her eyes)*	+ Teases him nonverbally, letting him know she supports him.
Kevin *(smiling)*: What? Come on. I've got to think it!	+ Accepts her support, joins in the teasing.
Suzanne *(still smiling)*: Of course.	+ Shows she accepts him, even though he's tight with money.
Kevin: On the other hand, it makes me hopeful, because what is life all about? Is it about paying off my debts? Hell, no. It should be about you and me, standing in the backyard wondering where to plant the zucchini.	+ Breakthrough statement of optimism. + Lets her know that enjoying life together is what really matters to him.
Suzanne: You know, naming things always is the first step. Now we know there's a problem and we can work on it together. It explains what's been going on, and that's a relief.	+ Expresses her support for him; her willingness to work as a team. + Validates his optimism. + Expresses her relief.

What They Say	What We Notice
Kevin: Well, it gives us a kind of a backdrop to look at things with different eyes.	+ Acknowledges they're on the same side.
Suzanne: Yeah, that's right. And you know, I also want to go on to talk about my own health issues, OK?	+ Validates his statement. + Brings up her own needs.
Kevin: Sure. I was thinking about how I feel about your blood disorder. Quite honestly, it scares me. And the scary thing about that is that I won't be there for you. Or that I'm *not* there for you.	+ Responds to her request to talk about her needs. + Expresses his worries about her health and his ability to support her. – Turns his attention back to himself and his own problem rather than focusing on her feelings.
Suzanne: What do you mean?	+ Asks for clarification.
Kevin: That I can't—that I won't rise to that challenge. Whatever that challenge is.	+ He gives her the clarification.
Suzanne: And I was wondering, what if it was the other way around? What if you were sick? I think I'd be scared a lot. I get terrified just when you tell me you're fatigued.	+ Shows she understands and empathizes. + Shares her feelings.
Kevin: Right.	+ Hears her.
Suzanne: Because . . .	+ This interruption looks like a problem, but he seems to finish her sentence just as she would have. Shows they're on the same page.

continued

What They Say	What We Notice
Kevin: What could it be?	
Suzanne: Yeah. But, you know, you never show that you worry about me. But sometimes I do wonder. I kind of want to poke you and say, "Is it just me? Or are you worrying here, too?"	+ Expresses her loneliness. + Expresses her need for him to be concerned about her and to express that.
Kevin: I'm worrying.	+ Responds to her need, lets her know he cares.
Suzanne: Because when we answered the questionnaires, I wasn't able to put down anything about the future. Every day I wonder, how long? Am I facing death? Were you thinking the same?	+ Goes further, telling him her deepest fears. + Asks about his feelings.
Kevin: No, but I think my life is sort of a living purgatory. I'm not so much worried about dying prematurely—I'm more worried about living too long.	− Doesn't respond to her fears. + Honest response, telling her the difference between being depressed and worrying about his own health.
Suzanne: Hmm.	+ Hears him.

Suzanne does just what we've advised her to do in this conversation: She makes a brave attempt to address her own needs by talking about her illness. Afterward, she tells us that she feels "a little frustrated" by the outcome; she isn't sure that Kevin really listened and understood.

Her response makes sense, we tell her. Kevin does seem to have a hard time shifting his focus to her experience. That's why they both need to pay attention to the balance of concern in their relationship.

At the same time, they also need to be patient with each other and their process. After seven years of sidestepping important issues, "you both have so much you need to say," explains Julie.

"It's like you've opened up whole new territories of conversation—your fears, your regrets, your values, your dreams," adds John. "It's going to take some time to fully explore all these areas."

We see lots of reasons to be optimistic about their future, we tell them. Some couples, after years of avoiding difficult issues, feel they have nothing to share with each other. That's not true for Kevin and Suzanne, who both express a desire to know each other at a deeper level. "There's so much going on for you," John marvels. "There's so much for you to talk about."

One Year Later

After our session, Kevin made an appointment with a therapist and started getting treatment for his depression, including antidepressants. As the clouds of sadness and lethargy started to lift, he felt motivated to become more physically active, so he joined a gym and started exercising daily. After about six months, he found he no longer needed the medication to keep his spirits up. Now he's off the antidepressants and he feels he has more energy than he's had in years. He's enjoying his job. He has taken up guitar—a pastime he'd set aside years ago. He's even changing his attitude about money. He recently bought himself a new guitar—a purchase that seemed far too frivolous a year ago. And as a result of his new, more liberal attitude toward spending, he and Suzanne are having fewer arguments about finances.

Because Kevin is less withdrawn, he and Suzanne are finding it easier to get along. Still, the couple has challenges ahead—including Suzanne's chronic illness. "I go through rough periods when I'm not feeling well and I get real controlling and grouchy," she explains. Both partners say they'd like to get better at sharing their feelings and comforting each other at times like this. And now that Kevin's depression has improved, they feel optimistic that they could benefit from couple's therapy. They've made an appointment with a marriage therapist to start sessions soon. "We're hoping that going to therapy will make us talk and hear each other better," says Suzanne. "And I think that's going to help immensely."

Helping Your Partner Through Depression

In their first dialogue, Kevin uses the common metaphor of an "eight-hundred-pound gorilla" to describe his depression. Suzanne, who had been subtly avoiding the topic, suddenly gets it. The depression is a third party in their marriage that must be acknowledged. If they keep trying to ignore it, things will only get worse.

Seeing depression as a third party is valuable because it allows partners to quit blaming themselves or each other for problems depression can cause. It compels them to face those problems, to empathize with each other, and to start working together for solutions.

Unfortunately, many people have a hard time admitting, or even recognizing, when they're depressed. This can be especially true for men, who are often raised to deny their feelings. When they experience the emotional emptiness or numbness that can be part of depression, they may not realize anything's wrong. On the other hand, a man may feel ashamed to admit that he *is* feeling down—that anxiety, sadness, or fatigue are keeping him from being productive at work, from enjoying leisure-time activities, or from getting excited about sex. Such feelings can conflict with a man's desire to see himself as a good provider, a good husband, and a good lover. Consequently, he may try to keep his negative emotions hidden. Meanwhile, his wife is in the dark, left to wonder why he's becoming increasingly irritable or withdrawn. Under these circumstances, it's common for wives to react as Suzanne did—to start criticizing and trying to control their husbands' behaviors. She may be thinking he's stubborn, lazy, or antisocial. But depressed? This may not occur to her.

In contrast, women are often more willing to admit to feeling sad or anxious. Still, many are reluctant to seek help because they're taught to believe that women are just naturally more emotional than men— that feeling "blue" or "bitchy" is just a normal part of a woman's life experience. They may blame their sadness on premenstrual syndrome (PMS), menopause, or other hormonal fluctuations that can cause normal changes in mood.

But depression—an unrelenting sadness or anxiety that continually blocks your ability to feel happiness and satisfaction with everyday life—is *not* normal for men or women. It's a mood disorder that can be caused by a chemical imbalance and made worse by stress or grief. The good news is that depression often can be treated successfully with counseling or medication, or both. Changes in lifestyle—such as exercising more and learning to manage daily stress—can also help.

Symptoms of Depression

- *A persistently sad, anxious, or "empty" mood.*
- *Feelings of hopelessness.*
- *Feelings of guilt, worthlessness, helplessness.*
- *Loss of interest or pleasure in hobbies and activities that you once enjoyed, including sex.*
- *Decreased energy, fatigue (like wearing concrete shoes).*
- *Difficulty concentrating, remembering, making decisions.*
- *Sleeping too much, or not being able to sleep.*
- *Loss of appetite or weight loss.*
- *Overeating and weight gain.*
- *Thoughts of death or suicide; suicide attempts.*
- *Restlessness.*
- *Irritability, grouchiness, being overly critical.*
- *Persistent physical symptoms that don't respond to treatment, such as headaches, digestive disorders, and chronic pain.*

If you suspect that your partner is depressed, here are some steps you can take together to prevent the condition from harming your marriage:

Encourage your partner to talk to a doctor or mental health professional.

Increasingly more health-care professionals are prepared to help their patients with depression. Tell your partner there's no shame in asking for help, and there's a lot to gain from feeling better.

Once diagnosed, encourage your partner to stick with treatment.

While there are many effective ways to treat depression, not all medications or therapies are effective for all people. In addition, some of the most common therapies—such as antidepressants—often take several weeks to start working. On top of this, people with depression can be easily discouraged. So you may need to give your spouse extra encouragement to continue treatment, or be willing to try new therapies if one approach doesn't seem to be working.

Learn to recognize and talk about the way depression affects your relationship.

There may be times when your spouse seems especially irritable or withdrawn. If you can understand these behaviors as symptoms of depression, it may prevent you from feeling rejected or hurt.

Help your partner stay safe.

Be aware that severe depression can lead to suicide. Check in with your partner about his or her feelings of hope or hopelessness. If you sense that your spouse is thinking about suicide, seek help from a therapist or crisis line right away.

Make sure the kids' needs are met.

Children shouldn't be burdened by a parent's depression. So take a close look at the kids' needs—especially if the depressed parent is their primary caretaker. Does that parent have enough energy, emotionally and physically, to respond to the children in kind, positive ways? Do you get the sense that the kids are caring for the parent instead of the other way around? If so, you may need to make other arrangements—such as having another adult care for the children while the depressed mom or dad gets treatment.

Respond to your spouse with empathy, while stating your own needs.

If your partner becomes harsh and critical, for example, you might reply, "It feels like your depression is talking now. Can you be a little gentler with me?" Or, if your spouse seems withdrawn, you might say, "I know you don't feel like connecting right now, but I need to tell you that I'm feeling lonely." Stating your needs in this way gives your spouse an opportunity to reassure you that, yes, he or she does care, and no, the issue is not personal. At the same time, you're letting your spouse know that you understand and care about what he or she is going through, as well.

Connect by touching.

Sometimes couples can connect through the emotional fog of depression via touch. Try hugging, cuddling, or massage as a way to comfort your spouse when he or she is feeling down. Avoid making sexual demands if your spouse isn't interested. Just focus on providing comfort and support.

Quiz: Are You Depressed?

Below is a list of problems and complaints that most people have from time to time. Read the list and rate each item based on how much discomfort that problem has caused for you in the past week, including today. Use this following scale of 0 to 4. **0** = Not at all, **1** = A little bit, **2** = Moderately, **3** = Quite a bit, **4** = Extremely

- Loss of sexual interest or pleasure   _____

- Feeling low in energy or slowed down   _____

- Thoughts of ending your life   _____

- Crying easily   _____

- Feelings of being trapped or caught   _____

- Blaming yourself for things   _____

- Feeling lonely   _____

- Feeling blue   _____

- Worrying too much about things   _____

- Feeling no interest in things   _____

- Feeling hopeless about the future   _____

- Feeling everything is an effort   _____

- Feeling worthless   _____

Total: _____

Find your score by dividing the total by 13:   _____

If your score is higher than 1.5, you may be depressed. If you find this mood persists for more than two weeks or so, talk to your doctor or a mental health counselor about your symptoms. (*Source: Symptom Checklist 90,* by Leonard R. Derogatis.)

Quiz: Are You Anxious?

Here's another list of problems and complaints that most people have occasionally. Read the list and rate each item based on how much discomfort that problem has caused for you in the past week, including today.

Use the following scale of 0 to 4. **0** = Not at all, **1** = A little bit, **2** = Moderately, **3** = Quite a bit, **4** = Extremely

- Nervousness or shakiness   ____

- Trembling   ____

- Suddenly scared for no reason   ____

- Feeling fearful   ____

- Heart pounding or racing   ____

- Feeling tense or keyed up   ____

- Spells of terror or panic   ____

- Feeling so restless you can't sit still   ____

- Feeling that something bad is going to happen to you   ____

- Frightening thoughts and images   ____

Total: ____

Find your score by dividing the total by 10:   ____

If your score is higher than 1.24, you may be anxious. If you find this mood persists for more than two weeks or so, talk to your doctor or a mental health counselor about your symptoms. (*Source: Symptom Checklist 90,* by Leonard R. Derogatis.)

Exercise: Establish a Ritual for Stress-Reducing Conversation

Research shows that one of the best things a couple can do for their marriage is to establish a ritual of regular conversation for coping with everyday stress and occasional sadness. This is the time—ideally each day—when you catch up, focus on each other, swap stories, and show support.

Such conversations can help you to manage pressure, anxiety, and sadness due to problems at your job or in difficult relationships with relatives and friends. These talks can be especially helpful if one or both of you struggle with depression as Kevin did. And even if your mood is generally upbeat, meaningful conversations can help you to handle life's challenges while staying emotionally connected. Think of it as being like a regular trip to the bank; your goal here is to make deposits in your "emotional bank account."

Use the following instructions and questions to design a conversation ritual for you and your partner. Try it a few times and then evaluate how it's going. Make adjustments as needed to design a ritual that works for you.

1. Designate fifteen to thirty minutes each day to talk about your day.

You may already do this to some extent. But we suggest that you make it intentional. You may want to attach the conversation to some other activity that you do day in and day out—something like eating breakfast together, commuting, taking a walk, or sharing coffee after dinner. The idea is to commit to making the conversation a *significant part* of that experience.

What is the best time of day for you to have a stress-reducing conversation with your partner? _____

Where is the best place to have it? _____

2. Do it the same way every time.

Examples: Sit at the same table, light a candle, use the same two matching coffee mugs. The idea is to make it feel like "a ritual," something you do together every day to feel connected to each other.

What elements will you use in your conversation ritual? _____

_____

3. Eliminate distractions.

Turn off the television. Let the phone ring. If you have small children, arrange for them to be involved in some other activity (sleeping is nice) so Mom and Dad can talk.

How will you make sure you've got each other's full attention? _____

_____

4. Take turns talking and listening.

Discuss the most important things that have happened to you since the last time you talked. What transpired at work? What did the doctor say? How was your class? Did you talk to your mom? Make sure that each partner gets equal time to talk about his or her day. At first, you can use a clock to time it. Later on, sharing the floor will come naturally.

What are likely topics for each of you in these conversations? _____

_____

5. Show support for your partner as you listen.

- Demonstrate genuine interest by asking questions: "How did it go?" "What was the most important part?" "How do you feel about that?" "What did that mean to you?" "Tell me everything that happened."

- Communicate understanding: "I can understand why you feel that way." "I'd be stressed out, too." "So it sounds like you're worried."

- Listen for emotion and respond in kind: "That's really sad." "I can see why you're angry." "Wow, that's exciting!" "I'd be tense in that situation, too."

- Celebrate your partner's success: "That's wonderful!" "I'm so proud of you!" "I'll bet you're so relieved."

169

- Take your partner's side in conflicts: "That guy is a total jerk." "How could she treat you like that?" (Remember, this is not the time for the listener to complain or criticize the speaker. And don't side with the enemy!)

- Show solidarity: "This is our problem and we will face it together." "I can understand because something similar happened to me."

- Be affectionate: "Come here and let me hold you." "I'm totally on your side."

- Offer help with problem solving: "Let's figure this out." But remember, understanding must come before advice. Don't rush to problem solve. Listening is the most important part.

6. Evaluate your experience.

After practicing a few days, analyze how the conversation is working. Ask these questions:

- Is the time and place working out for you?

- If not, do you need to make adjustments to your schedule so you can make it work?

- Are you able to avoid distractions?

- Are there any elements you'd like to add to make it more satisfying?

- Do you feel that your partner is sharing his or her experiences?

- Do you feel that your partner is listening to you?

What changes, if any, would you like to make in your ritual? _____

CHAPTER 7

"I Shouldn't Have to Nag!"

Growing up, Craig dreamed of marrying a woman like Beth—somebody he described as fiery, demonstrative, passionate. "I always believed a woman like that could awaken those qualities in me," the thirty-four-year-old machinist from Milwaukee explains. "So when I saw Beth, she excited me."

The two had met nine years earlier in Miami, where Beth was waiting tables to put herself through graduate school. Craig had escaped the winter weather to vacation in Florida with friends.

Beth, now thirty-nine, was instantly attracted to Craig as well. "I couldn't believe I met this guy who was not only handsome and smart—he was also extremely funny!" she remembers.

Their romance flourished through letters, short visits, and long telephone calls. Intense, time-limited conversations heightened the experience. "We felt as if we were looking into each other's essence," Craig recalls.

They got married just six months later, even though Craig's job and Beth's schooling kept them living in separate states. Then, after nearly a year of long-distance marriage, Beth moved to Wisconsin.

"It was immediate culture shock!" says Craig. Both fiercely

independent, the two faced off over issues of finances and where to live—conflicts that are still unresolved. Beth believes Craig is careless with money, while Craig feels Beth holds the purse strings too tight. Beth dislikes the harsh Wisconsin winters, and would like to move back to Florida. But Craig can't imagine leaving his family, his friends, and his job at the auto plant, where he revels in his role as union steward.

But the couple's most serious disputes center on household chores—an area of conflict that's grown increasingly contentious since their son Skylar was born five years ago. Because Beth usually works part-time as a fund-raiser for a charitable organization, the couple has agreed that she should do most of the housework and child care. But her workload at the office is often unpredictable, and sometimes she needs Craig's help with chores like laundry, cooking, and cleaning. Craig says he doesn't mind pitching in, but he needs reminders.

What's the Problem?

- *Beth opens conversations with criticism, sarcasm, or contempt—i.e., "harsh start-up."*
- *Craig reacts defensively.*
- *He is unwilling to accept her influence.*
- *Her self-critical thoughts and feelings of unworthiness block her ability to accept his appreciation and help.*

What's the Solution?

- *For Beth: "Soften start-up."*
- *For Craig: Be open to her influence.*
- *Express more appreciation.*
- *For Beth: Accept the compliments he offers.*

This irritates Beth because she feels Craig should be more attuned to their life together and what she needs. "I shouldn't have to nag!" she insists.

Lately their quarrels over housework have become so frequent and so painful that it's harming their marriage.

"The way we argue is disgusting!" laments Beth. "Whenever we get a moment to talk, something always blows up. So we end up wondering, 'Why do we even try to spend time together?' "

Craig recalls times when he and Beth felt much closer—when they bought their new house, for instance, or when his union went out on strike and Beth was so supportive. "We kind of rallied and worked together," he says. "It felt like we were on the same team, and that permeated everything—how we communicated and how we accepted each other. We felt fond of each other."

It hasn't been that way lately, though. These days he says he often views Beth as "hard" or "lashing out," rarely vulnerable. She's his adversary—"the person who is trying to make me spend less money, who is criticizing me because I don't work enough around the house," he says.

Even the humor has dissipated from their relationship, says Beth, sadly. Craig rarely laughs at her jokes anymore.

The couple also worries about the way their arguments may affect their son. Both say they'd like Skylar to see his parents respecting each other, discussing tough issues, and getting along. "But a lot of time he sees me as angry because I feel like I'm doing it all," says Beth.

Providing a better example for Skylar is important to both Craig and Beth, so we suggest that they try discussing their conflicts over housework with Skylar in mind.

Here's what happened:

What They Say	What We Notice
Beth: I want Skylar to grow up seeing teamwork. I want him to see us as the adults and himself the child—rather than seeing that I'm picking up after two kids. *(Pauses.)* You're smiling.	— Spoils a positive beginning with criticism and mild insult.

continued

What They Say	What We Notice
Craig: You've already referred to me as a kid.	+ Notices insult and gently tells her so.
Beth: Well, I sometimes feel that way—like I am cleaning up after two kids.	− Softens her complaint, but continues criticism; ends up defensive.
Craig: And I think we've got to work this stuff out so that it's not played out in front of Skylar.	+ States his complaint. + Takes some responsibility by saying "we."
Beth: I'd like to be able to say, "Can you vacuum?" without having you continue to type on the computer. We got into a fight about this on Saturday because I didn't say, "Can you vacuum *now?*"	− Ignores his complaint. + Expresses her need, her complaint.
Craig: You asked if I could vacuum, and the vacuuming got done.	− Defensive.
Beth: Right. And by the time I asked you to vacuum, I was totally frustrated because I had already scrubbed two tubs, three sinks, and two toilets—and I had to go to work. You want me to ask you to do things. But it's beyond me why I need to ask you to participate in cleaning up messes that we both make.	− Doesn't give him credit for vacuuming. − States complaint in a critical way, which escalates the argument. − Sarcasm (a form of contempt).
Craig: Well, I do participate. You describe feeling fed up, but I think you should ask for help before it gets that far.	− Defensive. +/− States his need, but uses "you should" rather than a request.

What They Say	What We Notice
Beth: I feel like it's going to start a fight.	+ Expresses her fear.
Craig: Give me an example of a time.	+ Asks for more information.
Beth: When I was carrying the dresser upstairs, you sat on the computer. And I said, "Can you help me?" We're talking about a dresser! Not like a little jewelry box. It was a *dresser!*	+ Expresses her feelings. − Harsh, accusing tone.
Craig: OK. Then what happened?	+ Asks for more information.
Beth: I said, "Can you help me carry this dresser upstairs?" Not a common request. And you said, "I'm in the middle of something." So I took the damned drawers out, and then carried this freaking dresser upstairs by myself. And you sat there. I felt like, "I cannot believe this man will not move and help me carry this dresser!" And then I saw that you were playing a baseball game on the computer! I thought you were doing something important for work!	+/− Expresses her complaint and her feelings about it, but does it in a harsh, accusing way.
Craig: Well, there's the issue of "I need you to do this" versus "I need you to do this *now.*"	− Doesn't acknowledge her frustration. +/− Stays calm, but defensive.
Beth: I get the feeling you hate the word *now.*	+ Probes for information about his feelings.

continued

What They Say	What We Notice
Craig: No, I've actually requested that you use the word *now* so that I understand. So that if I am in the middle of something, I can say, "I really can't help you now. I can help you in ten minutes."	− Defensive at first. + Clarifies his need.
Beth: Right. And I thought, "OK, it's hard for me to ask, but I'm going to ask." And then when you said, "I'm busy right now and I'll help you later," I took it as a slap in the face—like I'm not important enough for you to put down what you're doing.	− Doesn't respond to his stated need. + Reminds him how hard it is for her to ask for his help. + Clearly communicates how his refusal to help makes her feel.
Craig: But you *are* important. And I do want to help you. That's why I'm trying to identify if something needs to be done *now*.	+ Reassures her that she is important. + Tells her what he needs.
Beth: Can we just assume that I mean now? If I'm asking you, I mean *now!*	− Ignores his statement that he cares. − Ignores his stated need again. − Harsh tone escalates the conflict.
Craig: But do you understand that I have a flow in my life? You could have said, "Is now a good time to carry a dresser up the stairs?"	− Defensive.
Beth: And so what if it's not a perfect time?	− Ignoring his need. − Contemptuous.

What They Say	What We Notice
Craig: Well, I'm not asking for a perfect time.	– Defensive.
Beth: It feels like you are.	– Continues conflict.
Craig: No. I want communication and understanding. I want to be able to say, "Excuse me, I'm right in the middle of this thing"— even if it's just a game. "I've played it for seven innings and I really don't want to walk out in the middle of it. Is two and a half minutes going to cause a big deal?"	– Defensive. + Clearly states his needs. – Won't budge toward her position; shows he won't be influenced by her.
Beth: And I could ask you the same question: "Is it really 'a big deal' if you miss these two innings?"	– Ignores his statement of need; restates her own instead. – Won't budge on his needs, either; they've reached an impasse.

Our Analysis: Harsh Words and Defensiveness Trump Good Intentions

Despite their anger and frustration, we see strengths in Beth and Craig's relationship. One is their sense of urgency; they're trying hard to make a connection—a sign that there's still a lot of love between them. Also, they both want to improve their marriage for Skylar's sake. This shows they believe the stakes are high, which may motivate them to make positive changes.

But where to begin? The top of their conversation holds some clues. Notice how Beth is barely out of the gate before she criticizes Craig by calling him a child. We call this tendency "harsh start-up," which is the habit of beginning your interactions with criticism or contempt. Our research shows that conversations that begin this way are doomed to failure. In fact, we found that we could predict the outcome of a fifteen-minute conversation 96 percent of the time based on what happened in the first three minutes. Consequently, it may not matter how much Beth wants to improve her marriage. If she starts a lot of her conversations with Craig by insulting him or hurting his feelings, they won't make much progress. And, indeed, Craig shows his discouragement early on. His smile is a gentle warning that things aren't going well. He tries a few times to turn the conversation around by refocusing on Skylar, stating his needs, and asking Beth questions. But as Beth's criticism continues and intensifies, he becomes more and more resistant to anything Beth says. From this defensive position, he offers no indication that he's open to Beth's perspective. In other words, he's not about to agree that he should help with the housework without being asked. And his refusal to accept Beth's influence on this issue makes Beth even more frustrated and critical, sending them into an escalating spiral of attack-and-defend.

Another complicating factor is that Beth has a hard time accepting Craig's attempts at kindness. When he says, "You *are* important," for instance, it goes right by her. We suspect she's clinging to so much left-over resentment from years of arguing that it's drowning out Craig's positive words. Also, we learn in our interview with Beth and Craig that she carries lots of self-criticism and feelings of unworthiness because of childhood experiences.

"It sounds like you were raised to believe that you don't deserve praise," Julie observes. "So even when Craig compliments you, you don't accept those words. No matter what he says, you still feel crummy."

"It's a form of self-protection," John explains. "If you were raised with lots of criticism, you may feel vulnerable when somebody says something nice to you. You feel afraid that if you open yourself up to that kindness, you might also be opening yourself up to get slammed. So you try not to expect much."

Those same feelings of low self-regard have led Beth to believe she doesn't really deserve to ask for Craig's help, we discover. She equates asking for help with negative behavior on her part—-in other words, "nagging."

The trouble is, she really does feel overwhelmed with work at times. When that happens, she wishes Craig would just offer his help and save her from turning into a nag. (Remember, "nag" is her perception, not his.) When he doesn't offer help, she becomes resentful and angry toward Craig—feelings she expresses just as she learned as a child—through criticism and contempt.

Beth tells us she's aware of her critical nature and its origin, and she often makes resolutions to be kinder toward Craig.

"That usually lasts four or five days," Craig explains.

"Then I go back to being a witch," adds Beth.

In his defense, Craig responds quickly, "*I'm* not calling you that."

Meanwhile, Julie sees the opportunity for insight: "Is that how you see yourself?" she asks Beth.

"I think I do," says Beth sadly. Then she adds, "I'm a good person with a good heart, and I really do care. And I start off trying to be positive, but we just . . ." Her voice trails off as she makes a big, sweeping downhill gesture with her right hand.

"I get to feeling so hopeless," Beth adds, turning to Craig. "And I have this fear that one day you'll get so fed up with me, you'll just up and leave."

This confession takes Craig by surprise. "I don't feel that way. Even in tough times, I feel that we're going to hang in there," he says. "And I hope that the day will come when you feel that way, too."

Our Advice

To help Beth and Craig build more hope and confidence in their marriage, we suggest some basic changes in the way they interact.

1. PRACTICE "SOFTENED START-UP"

First, we advise Beth to use "softened start-up" rather than "harsh start-up" when she talks to Craig about their conflicts. That is, she needs to bring up her complaints to Craig in a more neutral, less accusing way. There's nothing wrong with saying, "I felt angry when you sat at the computer while I carried the dresser up the stairs." Indeed, Beth needs to let Craig know when his behavior upsets her. But her intensely critical, sarcastic tone is getting in the way of her message.

2. BE OPEN TO YOUR PARTNER'S INFLUENCE

Craig, on the other hand, needs to be more open to Beth's influence. Many people have trouble accepting their partner's ideas, suggestions, or requests because they believe that doing so will cause them to lose power in the relationship. However, our research has shown that just the opposite is true—especially for men. Husbands who allow themselves to be influenced by their wives actually have more power in their marriages than men who don't. That's because wives who feel empowered and respected in their marriages are more likely to go along with their husband's ideas and suggestions as well.

People who allow themselves to be influenced by their partners stop creating obstacles for each other and learn to compromise. We refer to this attitude as "the Aikido principle" because it's based on the same rule that's used in this modern Japanese martial art—that you must yield to your opponent in order to win. As paradoxical as it may seem, you become more powerful by sharing your power with others.

Craig's willingness to accept Beth's influence may also help her to become less frustrated and angry with Craig, so that she would be less likely to use harsh start-up when she's upset. In fact, our research also shows that when men share power in their marriages, their wives are far less likely to be critical and contemptuous toward their husbands.

So, what would this look like for Craig and Beth? It might mean that Craig would actually agree to some of the conditions that Beth is asking for. He might, for example, commit to vacuuming on weekends *even if she doesn't remind him to do so.*

3. TELL YOUR PARTNER WHAT YOU NEED

We also suggest that Beth be very explicit with Craig when she feels she needs him to be more open to her ideas and requests. She might say things like these:

- *"I really need you to listen to me right now."*

- *"I need to feel that what I say to you matters."*

- *"I need you to accept my influence in this situation."*

4. EXPRESS AND ACCEPT APPRECIATION

In addition, we suggest that both Craig and Beth show much more appreciation for each other. Our session revealed that they harbor a lot of resentment toward each other for past arguments and disappointments. The best way to move beyond such pain is to express gratitude for all the positive things you see in your partner. Your compliments don't have to be elaborate. They can be simple, frequent statements of positive things you notice in the moment. Examples might be:

- *"I like that color on you."*

- *"You were so patient when Skylar needed help with his math."*

- *"You had the oil changed in the car today? That's great that you remembered."*

Of course, expressing gratitude is just one part of the equation. The other is to hear and accept your partner's appreciation—rather than deny or ignore it, which Beth so often does. To help her change this pattern, we suggest that Craig keep offering his appreciation even when she pushes it away. And when she does so, he might remind her to stop, listen to his words, and "take it in." The goal is for Beth to learn to feel and believe all the good things about herself that Craig sees in her.

"It's hard to listen with new ears, to censor the self-criticism, and open yourself up to more positive messages," John explains. "But, over time, we believe the practice of offering and accepting positive, caring messages will make a difference. Your fondness for each other will grow, and your anger and criticism will diminish."

Here's what happens when Craig and Beth try the conversation again, using our suggestions:

What They Say	*What We Notice*
Beth: I've been working twice as many hours as I'm used to working. And I've been feeling overwhelmed with housework. I need some help to figure out how I can get more help from you without feeling like I'm nagging.	+ Good "softened start-up." + Great statement of feelings, describing the situation and her needs. + Makes request without blaming.
Craig: OK. I've seen that you're doing a lot more with your job. And I know how it feels to be overwhelmed. I think it would be really great if we could talk about both getting what we need. So tell me what you need.	+ Acknowledges her contribution. + Expresses understanding of her behavior and her feelings. + Expresses willingness to listen and work on the problem.
Beth *(laughs, exasperated)*: I just told you. I want to figure out a way to split the housework in a more equal fashion without my having to continually ask for help. Can we just set up a list of chores and commit to what we'll do? Would that work for you?	− Slightly critical, impatient response. − Doesn't give him credit for willingness. + Clarifies her request. + Makes a suggestion. + Asks him a question about his needs.

What They Say	What We Notice
Craig: Well, I think a list can be a good idea. And I think it's important for you to be willing to ask for help as well. Because I'm concerned that I'm not going to be able to give you everything you need without some reminders from you.	+ Gives her credit for asking for help. + Shows some willingness to accept her idea. + Expresses honest fear that he's going to let her down.
Beth: Well, how about if we just make a list and put a copy on the refrigerator where we can both see the load that we're supposed to be carrying?	− Doesn't respond directly to his concern about her suggestion. + She makes the proposal more concrete.
Craig: OK. I think a list is a good idea.	+ He finally agrees, accepting her influence. + He compliments her idea.
Beth: Thank you. *(She smiles sweetly, playfully.)*	+ Expresses pleasure that he's responded to her suggestion. (Playful attitude helps a lot.) + She accepts his appreciation.
Craig *(smiling, too)*: You're welcome. I also want it to be OK for you to ask for help. So if the list isn't totally working the way that you'd like it to work, it's OK for you to remind me. I don't view it as nagging. I want you to understand that I care. I see all the work that you do around the house and I think it's awesome.	+ Shows even more willingness to support her. + Repeats his need for verbal reminders. + Expresses that he cares. + Expresses more appreciation.

continued

What They Say	What We Notice
Beth: It feels really good to hear you say that right now. And I think I need to hear it periodically. I know you can't do that all the time—like, "Wow, that toilet is really sparkling today!" But if I hear it, I feel like my effort is not a waste of my time.	+ She "takes in" his appreciation. + Expresses her need to hear it. + Her humor continues to help.
Craig: Right. And I think that's reasonable. And for all the work that you do around the house, I think that you deserve that.	+ Responds to her expressed need. + Continues appreciation.
Beth: Should I ask for it?	+ Asks for information.
Craig (hesitantly): No.	+ Honest response.
Beth: Because you hate it when I ask for a compliment.	+ Probes for more understanding of his feelings.
Craig: No, I'm going to give you my best pledge that it's going to come without your having to try to remind me. Because I feel that prompted appreciation seems somewhat hollow.	+ Responds by clarifying his commitment and feelings. + Promises to meet her need.
Beth: So you want to be reminded about the chores.	+ Validates his need and shows she understands.

What They Say	What We Notice
Craig: Yes, and I want you to understand that you deserve the right to ask for help. I want you to understand that I want to help.	+ Responds. + Tells her he values her. + Expresses willingness to help.
Beth: Do you swear?	+ Asking for reassurance.
Craig: I swear.	+ He gives it.
Beth: And I'm going to work on feeling more worthy of asking and not worrying that you're going to get mad.	+ Shows that she took in his healing words. + Expresses willingness to do her part.
Craig: This conversation makes me hopeful. I think this will also feed into what Skylar sees.	+ Expresses optimism. + Reminds her of their shared goal (to be better role models for their son).
Beth: Right.	+ Expresses agreement.

At the end of our session, Craig and Beth feel optimistic—especially when it comes to Skylar.

"I think of standing in the kitchen and you coming up behind me and giving me a hug," Beth tells Craig. "That would be nice for Skylar to see."

"What a great way to state your needs," John points out. "You could have said it this way: 'You'd never think of just coming up to me in the kitchen and giving me a hug, would you?' The way you just stated it was so much better!"

Beth accepts the compliment. But then she worries that it won't be easy to change. "That last conversation felt contrived. I had to keep telling myself, 'I am *not* going to be negative.'"

"It will feel like that for a while because your instincts tell you that the negative statements are 'the truth' and therefore you should state it," Julie explains.

"But it's not necessary, is it?" says Beth.

"It's really not," says Julie. "And it's not helpful."

"There will always be times when either of you are negative, harsh, or defensive," warns John. "These are well-worn grooves. But when it happens, don't feel like it's a lost cause. You can turn it around. And over time, if you find that it's happening in just 30 percent of your conversations instead of 90 percent of your conversations, that's a huge improvement!"

One Year Later

Our follow-up interview reveals that Craig and Beth's marriage has improved in much the way John predicted it would. The couple reports that their efforts to share more appreciation have made a big difference.

"We're getting better at saying, 'Thanks for doing this,' or 'Hey, I noticed that,'" says Craig. "We still have our meltdowns, but they're less severe and they last for a shorter duration. And we used to hold grudges afterward, which creates a kind of funk over the house. Now there's less damage being done when we tend to recover quicker."

"We're making more deposits in our emotional bank account," Craig adds, referring to a concept they learned about at one of our workshops. The idea is to keep a tally of all the specific steps you take to connect in positive ways throughout the day. These might include phone calls, favors, compliments, signs of physical affection. You don't track them in order to compete. Rather, you do it to make sure that you're creating an ample supply of fondness and good feelings toward each other. This surplus of positive regard can really come in handy when it's time to face the conflicts that inevitably come up.

Beth says Craig is slowly getting better at accepting her ideas and suggestions. For example, she's the thrifty one in their partnership, so she has tried for years to persuade Craig to save his expensive dress shoes for special occasions. "It just doesn't make sense to me that you'd need to wear $150 shoes to take out the trash," she explains. So it was great for her to look out the window recently and see Craig mowing the lawn in his well-worn work shoes. With no prompting from her, he pointed to his shoes and yelled, "See? I'm accepting influence!"

Both Beth and Craig say they've still got lots of conflict in their marriage, and they've come to accept that many of their differences will always be there. This acceptance makes it feel like less of a struggle.

"We celebrated our tenth anniversary this summer, which was significant for both of us," Beth explains. "After a decade together, we know each other so much better. He does this stupid thing and I do that dumb thing. And you know what? It doesn't matter! We're still together!"

Quiz: Harsh Start-up: A Problem in Your Marriage?

Beth and Craig often got off to a bad start in discussing their conflicts because Beth had a habit of starting conversations with a statement of criticism or contempt. This "harsh start-up" made Craig feel so defensive that he wouldn't listen to Beth, which made her even more frustrated and angry—increasing the chance that she'd introduce her next complaint with criticism and contempt as well. This vicious cycle was making it nearly impossible for them to solve their problems.

The following questionnaire may help you determine if harsh start-up is harming your marriage:

PARTNER A		PARTNER B
T/F		T/F
_____	1. My partner is often very critical of me.	_____
_____	2. I hate the way my partner raises an issue.	_____
_____	3. Arguments often seem to come out of nowhere.	_____
_____	4. Before I know it, we're in a fight.	_____
_____	5. When my partner complains, I feel picked on.	_____
_____	6. I seem always to get blamed for problems.	_____
_____	7. My partner is negative all out of proportion.	_____
_____	8. I feel I have to ward off personal attacks.	_____
_____	9. I often have to deny charges leveled against me.	_____
_____	10. My partner's feelings are too easily hurt.	_____
_____	11. What goes wrong is often not my responsibility.	_____
_____	12. My spouse criticizes my personality.	_____
_____	13. Issues get raised in an insulting manner.	_____
_____	14. At times my partner complains in a smug or superior way.	_____
_____	15. I have just about had it with all this negativity between us.	_____
_____	16. I feel basically disrespected when my partner complains.	_____
_____	17. I just want to leave the scene when complaints arise.	_____
_____	18. Our calm is suddenly shattered.	_____
_____	19. I find my partner's negativity unnerving and unsettling.	_____
_____	20. I think my partner can be totally irrational.	_____

SCORING

Give yourself one point for each "true" answer.

If you score under five, harsh start-up is probably not a big problem in your marriage. You and your spouse initiate difficult discussions with little criticism or contempt. As a result, your chances for handling conflict are good.

If you scored over five, you're probably using too much criticism and contempt when you talk about problems. Taking a more gentle approach will improve your ability to handle conflict together. The following exercise may help.

Exercise: Turning Harsh Start-up to Softened Start-up

Our research shows that the way you start your conversations makes a big difference in the overall quality of your marriage. Harsh start-up—that is, beginning with criticism or contempt—causes the interaction to go downhill fast. Partners become defensive and withdraw, leading to emotional distance and loneliness. The opposite is softened start-up, which is free of criticism and contempt.

Below are five examples of common marital conflicts, followed by examples of harsh start-up and softened start-up.

1. The holidays are approaching and you're worried because your partner often spends more on her family than the two of you can afford.

HARSH START-UP: "I hate the holidays! Your shopping always drives us into debt."

SOFTENED START-UP: "I really want to enjoy the holidays with you this year. But I'm worried about the bills. Can we talk about a budget?"

2. Your partner likes to go to clubs with friends each weekend, but you like to spend more evenings at home together.

HARSH START-UP: "I'm sick of going out with your friends all the time."

SOFTENED START-UP: "I feel like spending time alone together. How about if I cook a nice dinner on Saturday and we stay home for a change?"

3. After a bad day at work, you come home to a headache, a messy house, and two quarreling kids. Your partner arrives, turns on the baseball game, and asks, "What's for dinner?"

HARSH START-UP: "How the hell should I know? And why do I always have to cook?!"

SOFTENED START-UP: "I don't know, and I don't feel very well. It would be great if you'd take care of dinner."

4. You'd like to make love tonight, but your partner's been distant. You wonder whether he even finds you attractive anymore.

HARSH START-UP: "What's wrong with your sex drive lately? You sure don't seem like the guy I married."

SOFTENED START-UP: "I've really been missing you. Remember how we made love at the cabin last summer? Tell me what I can do to get you interested."

Now, draft a list of conflicts that are common in your marriage. Then think of ways you might start a conversation with your partner about these issues, using softened start-up.

Here are few simple rules to remember as you begin:

- *Complain, don't criticize or blame.*

- *Start your sentences with "I" instead of "you."* (Example: I feel anxious when we're running late," versus "You never seem to get ready on time.")

- *Talk clearly about what you need.* (Example: "I need for us to agree on our budget" versus "I wish you'd quit wasting money.")

- *Be polite.*

- *Express appreciation.*

THE COMMON CONFLICT:_____

_____

SOFTENED START-UP: _____

THE COMMON CONFLICT:_____

_____

SOFTENED START-UP: _____

THE COMMON CONFLICT:_____

_____

SOFTENED START-UP: _____

THE COMMON CONFLICT:_____

_____

SOFTENED START-UP: _____

THE COMMON CONFLICT:_____

_____

SOFTENED START-UP: _____

Quiz: Are You Open to Your Partner's Influence?

Another problem we perceived in Beth and Craig's marriage was Craig's unwillingness to accept influence from Beth. Our research shows that this problem—which is most common among husbands—can be harmful to a relationship. That's because it leads wives to become frustrated and angry, increasing the chances that they'll become highly critical and contemptuous—behaviors proven to be quite destructive in a marriage.

To find out if accepting influence is a challenge in your marriage, answer the following questions:

PARTNER A		PARTNER B
T/F		T/F
____	1. I am really interested in my partner's opinions on our basic conflicts.	____
____	2. I usually learn a lot from my partner, even when we disagree.	____

191

PARTNER A		PARTNER B
T/F		T/F

_____   3. I want my partner to feel that what he or she says really matters to me.   _____

_____   4. I generally want my partner to feel influential in this marriage.   _____

_____   5. I can listen to my partner.   _____

_____   6. My partner has a lot of basic common sense.   _____

_____   7. I try to communicate respect, even during our disagreements.   _____

_____   8. If I keep trying to convince my partner, I will eventually succeed.   _____

_____   9. I don't reject my partner's opinions out of hand.   _____

_____   10. My partner is not rational enough to take seriously when we discuss our conflicts.   _____

_____   11. I believe in lots of give and take in our discussions.   _____

_____   12. I am very persuasive, and usually can win arguments with my partner.   _____

_____   13. I feel I have an important say when we make decisions.   _____

_____   14. My partner usually has good ideas.   _____

_____   15. My partner is basically a great help as a problem solver.   _____

_____   16. I try to listen respectfully, even when I disagree.   _____

_____   17. My ideas for solutions are usually much better than my partner's ideas.   _____

_____   18. I can usually find something to agree with in my partner's position.   _____

_____   19. My partner is usually too emotional.   _____

_____   20. I am the one who needs to make the major decisions in this relationship.   _____

SCORING: Give yourself one point for each "true" answer, except for items 8, 10, 12, 17, 19, 20. Then subtract one point for each "true" answer to items 8, 10, 12, 17, 19, 20. If you scored 6 or above, accepting influence is an area of strength in your marriage. If you scored below 6, you and your partner need to make improvements in your willingness to accept influence from each other.

Exercise: Using the Aikido Principle to Accept Influence

Couples who have trouble accepting influence from each other often argue and feel defensive. One partner makes a complaint or suggestion and the other responds with a statement of denial or refusal. In these situations, neither partner wants to admit he or she is wrong. Neither one wants to be in the shameful position of being "the loser." But the trouble is, the arguments that ensue can be harmful to your marriage.

An alternative to this deadlocked position is to accept influence. We refer to this as "the Aikido principle" because it involves a concept crucial to this Japanese form of martial art—that you must "yield to win." In other words, you don't go head-to-head with the person who is attacking you; you fall in line beside your partner instead. This can be done simply by asking your partner questions about his or her point of view and expressing willingness to look at the problem from a new perspective. Responses might be:

- Explain your thinking to me.

- What are all your feelings about this issue?

- Tell me why this is so important to you.

- Tell me how you would solve the problem if you were going to solve it alone.

- I may not be looking at it the same way you do. Tell me how you would approach this.

- What are you afraid of in this situation?

- What disasters are you trying to avoid?

- What are your goals around this issue?

- This seems to be important to you. Tell me why.

- Help me understand why you feel so strongly about this.

Responding in this way can be totally disarming—especially if your partner is poised for a fight. It changes the energy of the conversation, allowing the two of you to approach the conflict from the same perspective and build understanding. You may even find a compromise.

One reason the Aikido principle is so successful is that it restores dignity to the conversation and allows both partners to maintain their self-respect. There are no winners and losers in this kind of exchange. Partners can have different points of view, and that's OK.

The following chart shows a few examples of alternative responses to complaints and attacks. As you read them, imagine the different tracks the conversations might take, based on whether you choose to go head-to-head or to yield and be influenced. Which response do you think might lead to a closer relationship?

Your partner complains or attacks you.	You go head-to-head; you don't accept influence.	You yield to win; you accept influence.
I don't like you going out for drinks after work all the time.	I don't do it "all the time." I only go out on Fridays.	This seems to worry you. Tell me what you're afraid of.

Your partner complains or attacks you.	You go head-to-head; you don't accept influence.	You yield to win; you accept influence.
You told your mother we'd have Thanksgiving with her before you asked me what I wanted to do.	I'm sorry but you know how important Thanksgiving is to my mother.	I'm sorry. That was probably the wrong thing to do. What do you think we should do now?
You're spending way too much on clothes.	What do you know about fashion?	Maybe I don't think about spending money on clothes the same way you do. Let's talk about it.
They passed you over for a promotion again? I can't believe you put up with this!	Look, there's nothing I can do about it, so forget it!	It makes me unhappy, too. Do you have any suggestions?
Look at the mess you left in this bathroom. It drives me nuts!	You're upset because I left the towels on the floor? You're a lunatic!	Tell me why this bothers you so much.

Think about an argument you and your partner recently had or are likely to have in the future. Imagine how the conversation might go if one of you were to respond to the other's complaint or attack with a statement that accepts influence. Write down your imagined complaint/attack and your imagined response.

COMPLAINT OR ATTACK:_____

_____

Response that accepts influence:_____

COMPLAINT OR ATTACK:_____

_____

Response that accepts influence:_____

COMPLAINT OR ATTACK:_____

_____

Response that accepts influence:_____

COMPLAINT OR ATTACK:_____

_____

Response that accepts influence:_____

COMPLAINT OR ATTACK:_____

_____

Response that accepts influence:_____

COMPLAINT OR ATTACK:_____

_____

Response that accepts influence:_____

COMPLAINT OR ATTACK:_____

_____

Response that accepts influence:_____

Using the Aikido principle to accept influence may not come naturally at first. Most of us are much more conditioned to respond to complaints or attacks in a defensive way. But if you can stay calm and think creatively in the moment, a nondefensive response is possible. You may find the result so positive that you'll decide to make it a habit in the future.

CHAPTER 8

"There's No Passion, There's No Fun"

In fifty-one years of marriage, Jack and Maureen have tried to follow the old advice: "Accentuate the positive, eliminate the negative." So when Jack remembers meeting his sweet-natured bride at college in 1950, he focuses on his good fortune. "I always felt lucky that you agreed to marry me," he tells her.

But Maureen insists he's being too modest. "You were the plum in that year's senior class," she reminds him. "You could have had any girl on campus. I was the lucky one."

Such appreciation continues as they talk about all they've shared over the years. Both former social workers, they're grateful for their home, the three children they raised, their church community, and their good sense in saving for a comfortable retirement.

And yet, when pressed to describe the entire picture of their marriage, it's clear that both partners feel something's missing—and it has been for a long time.

"We have a warm affection for each other, but we're not very adventurous or fun loving," says Maureen, seventy-four. "We don't have a lot of passion or fun in our marriage."

"We're both quite shy in the bedroom," adds Jack, seventy-six.

What's the Problem?

- Maureen hides her anger.
- When she does talk about being mad, she focuses largely on the needs of others, not on her own.
- Jack often withdraws when Maureen gets angry.
- Ignoring Maureen's anger makes both feel emotionally distant—interferes with passion, fun, sexual response.

What's the Solution?

- For Maureen:
  - Identify and express what's making you angry.
  - Express anger in a more constructive way.
  - Express more appreciation of Jack.
- For Jack: Listen and respond to Maureen's anger.

"Maybe we were more uninhibited when we were younger."

"I don't think I ever felt uninhibited," Maureen says sadly. "I used to feel very sorry for myself about it, but I don't so much anymore."

Still, she longs for more emotional intimacy with Jack—a dream she still believes is possible. "I would like to reach a point where we're sharing feelings that we don't share now," she explains. "I think there are whole areas that we're afraid to express."

For example, when Maureen gets angry, she always tries to hide it from Jack. She's afraid that it would hurt their relationship, she explains. And, in fact, Jack has revealed in our questionnaire that he usually responds to Maureen's anger by withdrawing. He doesn't see any point in discussing difficult feelings.

"I think one of my big fears has been that if I looked at my anger honestly, it would result in a separation and that's not what we want," Maureen says as Jack nods in agreement.

But lately it's been getting harder for Maureen to keep her anger under wraps. They point to a recent incident in a church discussion group as an example. Maureen noticed that the men were monopolizing the conversation while all the women in this characteristically polite crowd passively listened. She had a sense that some of the women in the group wanted to share ideas, but they felt intimidated by a few domineering men in the group. This whole idea that her women friends were being silenced against their will started to eat at Maureen. So, after fuming silently for quite some time, she made a sudden angry comment, letting the whole group know how mad she was about the way they were behaving. "If we women were to break off and go somewhere else to meet, we'd be talking our heads off!" Maureen snapped at the man leading the discussion. Meanwhile, the rest of the group—including Jack—sat stunned and bewildered.

Maureen's outburst had repercussions. On the way home that night, Jack told her she had behaved inappropriately and it embarrassed him. And the next day the discussion leader sent Maureen an e-mail message saying she had hurt his feelings. As a result, Maureen made the difficult choice to quit attending the group.

At the same time, she noticed that acting out caused some positive ripples in her life. "Expressing myself in that painful situation, rather than just stuffing it down, made a difference in my physical response to Jack," Maureen explains. In other words, it somehow allowed her to feel sexier.

This doesn't surprise us, we tell her. Keeping a lid on your anger creates distance in a relationship, and that makes it hard to have fun together, to take risks emotionally and physically, and to enjoy sex. But if you use your anger to stand up for what you need, you gain self-respect, which is an important part of feeling free to express sexual feelings.

This makes sense to Maureen. "Sometimes I think that if Jack and I would fight more passionately, there would be more passion in our whole relationship, but I haven't been sure," she says.

Another good thing happened, says Maureen. After several weeks of absence, she got a note from a male friend in the group asking her to return. When she called to thank him, he told her he knew what she was going through. "It was the most wonderful conversation," She recalls. "Nobody has ever understood the kind of pain I was in the way that this man did."

"What if you could have a conversation with Jack that would make you feel that well understood?" John asks. "What if Jack could help you to open up in that way?"

"That's the kind of progress I was hoping we could make with your help," Maureen replies as Jack nods in agreement.

Because this incident seemed like such a turning point for Maureen and Jack, we suggested they discuss their feelings about it with each other. Here's an excerpt of that talk:

What They Say	*What We Notice*
Maureen: Do you have any understanding of what I've been trying to express?	+ Reaching out to him.
Jack: Well, I know that we've talked about men having both a masculine and feminine side and you said my feminine is kind of sub-merged or something.	+ Nice attempt to express under-standing, even though it reveals his confusion.
Maureen: No, Caroline said that in that dream class.	− Correction with a hint of criticism, resentment.
Jack: So I guess I need to get a clearer under-standing.	+ Admits he doesn't understand; still trying.

What They Say	What We Notice
Maureen: Well, when you and the other men get to talking, it seems to me that all awareness of what the other people are feeling is gone. I feel the speaker has a responsibility to be aware of the people in his or her audience.	+ Expresses her anger.
Jack: I suppose I could practice that.	+ Amazingly accepting.
Maureen: I'm going to risk something here, and I hope I don't pay for it later on. We were at the Smiths' Tuesday night, and the men spent all evening talking about experiences in World War II. On the way home, you said what a great time you had had. But I felt like my head was going to explode!	+ Takes a risk to tell him how strongly she feels about this. + Clearly complaining without criticizing.
Jack: Well, do you deny that some people have more to say than others? Take our book group, for example. We have a retired professor in the group. He has spent his whole career drawing from the literature, and . . .	− Defensive response.
Maureen: And therefore I'm supposed to be quiet because he has so much more to say?	+/− Expresses anger, but with slight sarcasm.
Jack: Well, yeah. That's what I'm asking.	+ Asking for clarification.

continued

What They Say	What We Notice
Maureen: Well, I don't see it that way. In fact, it even occurred to me that some people may feel too intimidated to speak up because we've got this expert in the room. If we're going to have a class and somebody's going to teach it, let's call it a class. But if we're going to have a club to discuss a book that everyone has a reaction to, let's make sure it's a conversation. Let's make sure that everybody has a chance to talk.	+ Continues expressing her feelings. − Distances herself from her anger by talking about the group instead of her own personal experience; relies on "we" instead of "I."
Jack: Well, it's a little mind-boggling to me that these women have remained passive and silent. I just have to assume—	+ Expresses his confusion honestly. − Somewhat defensive.
Maureen: It's because—(she catches herself for interrupting him and covers her mouth with her hand).	+ Stops herself from interrupting, a good repair.
Jack: It's because they're more interested in what one of the other speakers has to say than in expressing themselves. You're saying that's not the case and maybe they're just being passive out of habit.	+ Shows he's getting her point; does not take her criticism personally.
Maureen: I look around at these discussion groups and I see women my age who are of a certain kind. We're what I call "nice ladies." We don't want to be told we're "not nice." That would be pretty threatening. But I think there has got to be a different way of being in these groups other than just being a passive "nice lady."	+/− Taking more responsibility for her feelings, but still creating distance by talking about "we."

Our Analysis: Failure to Express Anger Leads to Emotional Distance

We see some very good things happening in this conversation. Although Jack shows a bit of defensiveness, he seems quite willing to hear Maureen's complaint and to accept her suggestions for fixing the problem. That's a tremendous advantage for this marriage.

Also, Maureen does a good job of describing her anger. But it would be better if she'd talk more about her *own* feelings in this situation rather than the needs of all the women in their group. We suspect that talking about the group's needs makes the conversation feel safer for both her and Jack. But it also puts some distance between them—and that may be the distance that she's most longing to cross.

Our Advice

We invite Jack and Maureen to think about how they can support each other to become more emotionally engaged.

For Jack, this means continuing to do what he's done in this first conversation—to keep talking and listening and responding—despite the fact that he may feel like withdrawing from the conversation when Maureen is angry.

To help Maureen go deeper in expressing her own personal feelings, we suggest that she take a closer look at what's happening in those moments when her anger first comes to the surface. She might ask, "What's my goal in this situation?" and "What's getting in my way of accomplishing that goal?"

This advice strikes a chord with her. "I have always been led to believe that anger is wrong and that I have no right to be angry, but I think that my anger has enabled me to get through things," she says.

"Do you believe that getting angry is a matter of preserving your dignity?" John guesses.

"That's correct, and I think I learned that as a child," she says, referring to a time when she was sexually abused by an older relative. "I simply got angry and closed everybody off. I decided, 'I'll make my

203

own way, thank you very much, and I'm not ever telling you how I feel again.' "

"So being angry became a matter of self-respect for you," says John.

"I think so," Maureen answers.

"And you don't respect being a compliant, 'nice lady' anymore?"

"No, I don't," she says.

"Would it mean a lot to you if Jack could support you in expressing your feelings in an open, honest way?"

"Yes, it would," she replies. "And when I say that something makes me angry, it doesn't mean that anybody's right or wrong. It's just what I'm feeling in the moment."

Jack, who's been listening intently, nods in agreement. He's taking in everything she says. In fact, he's been doing this throughout the session, demonstrating an extraordinary willingness to listen to her and to be influenced by her. In addition, he often offers her compliments.

What is Maureen's response to all this positive attention? While she's certainly respectful to Jack, we notice that she doesn't seem to acknowledge or appreciate his kind attention as much as she could. While Maureen tells *us* she really appreciates how Jack responds to her, we think it would do wonders for their relationship if she would tell *him*—moment by moment—that she notices the good things he says and does.

The pair agrees to take our advice as they return to the topic of the church discussion group.

What They Say	*What We Notice*
Maureen: I would like to see the person who is running the group check in with each person occasionally to see how they are feeling about the discussion.	+ Begins with constructive suggestion.

What They Say	What We Notice
Jack: So you would feel better if you had some positive support from me for that sort of thing. And I don't have any problem with that. I guess some of my problem is . . . *(He pauses to collect his thoughts.)* You know that when we got married fifty years ago, you may have been an angry person, but it was sure hidden underneath. Do you remember what my father said? "You've introduced us to a very sweet, gentle girl."	+ Expresses support. + Accepts influence. + Takes the conversation to a deeper, more personal level. + Expresses his confusion about the changes he's seen in her.
Maureen: In those days I wasn't in touch with my feelings.	+ Reframes his statement to clarify.
Jack: But now it's almost as if I'm married to a different person.	+ Expresses his feelings and confusion.
Maureen: That's right. It *is* almost as though you're married to a different person. And the more I try to be genuinely who I am, rather than what I think—or somebody else thinks—I *ought* to be, I run the risk of becoming somebody you don't like. And I think there are times that you don't like me.	+ Validates his feelings. + Talks about her own feelings rather than the group. + Expresses her fears and worries. + Great honesty.
Jack *(nodding, thoughtfully)*: Yeah. *(Long pause.)* To be perfectly candid, when you have an outburst of anger with a group of people who have gotten together to discuss religion—people we hardly know—I am nonplussed.	+ Honesty in return. + Validates her feelings. + Expresses his anger, embarrassment, fear.

continued

What They Say	What We Notice
Maureen: And that's why I need to learn a different way of expressing myself in those situations. I was attempting to be honest and I didn't do it very well. I've got to find a different way of expressing my anger. Through the years, it was always OK for *you* to be angry in the marriage.	+ Takes responsibility for the problem. +/− Expresses her feeling that their double standard about anger has been unfair; a bit critical, defensive, sarcastic.
Jack: Umhmmm.	+ Taking it in.
Maureen: You frequently were angry and expressed it in a male fashion.	− Still critical.
Jack: Ummhmm. Well. Yeah. There is that different cultural expectation. But I personally think I should avoid getting angry and I do to the greatest degree that I can. When I'm angry, I just head out for a walk and walk it off.	+ Shows he's listening. − A bit defensive.
Maureen: I suspect that that doesn't help us to get closer.	+ Clarifies what she wants from him—emotional intimacy.
Jack: No. Well, I told you after the meeting that I was upset. I made that pretty clear. I didn't just sit around and avoid talking about it.	+ Validates her need. − Still a little defensive.
Maureen: And that's why we were able to talk about it.	+ Points out their strength, their progress.

What They Say	What We Notice
Jack: So is there anything else I could do to be more positive and supportive of your needs with regard to . . . *(He pauses again.)* Well, I guess there's this whole business of the dining table, how you feel that with me always sitting at the head of the table, that you feel diminished.	+ Asking her what she needs. + Shows support for her goal of getting more respect.
Maureen: Yeah, it was never my intention of having that table. I wanted a round one.	+ Validating his thought; accepting his suggestion.
Jack: So would it be a move in the right direction to just get rid of that table? To sell it in a yard sale and get a round table?	+ Very supportive, showing he accepts her influence.
Maureen: *(Pauses and looks at him intently, with one eyebrow raised.)* Ummhmm. For me it would.	+ Expresses her amazement, and validates that he's on the right track.
Jack: Well, that's one indication of support. And I could do something about the book club on Sunday. But I don't want to move in and say, "From now on, we're going to do it this way."	+ Still supportive, while being realistic.
Maureen: No, that would be awkward. But I think it would be good to go around and give everybody a chance to talk.	+ Validates his realism. + Accepts his support.
Jack: Yeah. OK.	+ Reassures her that he means it.

In this second conversation, Jack and Maureen show great progress in their willingness to share deep feelings openly and honestly. They both reveal a little bit of defensiveness in this conversation, but they're talking about some very difficult issues here, so that's to be expected.

What truly impressed us was Jack's demonstration that he's paying attention to Maureen's feelings. When he suggests getting a new dining room table, he's showing Maureen, in a really concrete way, that he supports her goal of attaining more dignity and more respect. Maureen is also showing that she cares about Jack's feelings, especially when she admits that she should learn to express her anger in more constructive ways.

Although Maureen's appreciation for Jack doesn't surface in this conversation, it does appear later on as we're wrapping up our session.

"This really is what Jack is like," she tells us. "If I can just work up my courage to get across what I'm feeling—and if I can do that without making him feel like he's under attack—then he really comes through for me."

With that in mind, we encourage Maureen to keep being emotionally honest with Jack. And we encourage Jack to keep paying attention to Maureen—especially when she's angry.

"As surprising as this may sound, a wife's anger can be a real resource—particularly in a marriage like yours," says John. "It's a sign that Maureen's no longer deadening her responses. It's a sign that she's coming alive. And that can be the key to having much more passion and fun in this relationship."

One Year Later

Seated at their new, round dining room table, Maureen and Jack describe the shifts in their marriage over the past year as "a 180-degree change."

"Maureen has become more cheerful, more positive, and much more assertive," says Jack.

"And I think Jack is beginning to enjoy himself more. That's been very nice to see," says Maureen.

They both attribute much of the change to Maureen's conscious effort to tell Jack when she feels angry and why. Jack is grateful for Maureen's honesty because he's no longer in the dark about what's bothering her, and they can usually find solutions.

Here's just one of many examples: Jack recently rearranged a kitchen cupboard, moving some of his medication into a space Maureen was using for her pills. "Months ago, I would have stewed about how thoughtless he had been, but I wouldn't have said anything," says Maureen. "This time I told him how I felt. I said, 'This area is mine and I don't like it that you invaded my space.'" Then she got a chopstick and used it to divide the space, designating one area for her and one for him.

Jack's reaction? "I felt a little surprised, because I thought that part of the cupboard was just sort of a general area. But if she feels that way, that's OK. It seemed like a good, practical way to make sure that we didn't get into a snit."

"I'm learning that if I make myself clear, Jack is so willing to accommodate me," Maureen adds, smiling warmly at her husband. "And, lo, these fifty years, I missed all those opportunities to teach him!"

Maureen's also aware that she missed many opportunities to appreciate Jack. So now, "Instead of only seeing negative things about him, I have begun to see all the positive things," she reports. In fact, she's made a list of his attributes, which she shares with us. It includes words like *supportive, affectionate, accepting,* and *trusting.* Turning to him, she sees him beaming. "And when you're relaxed and smiling, you're quite handsome," she adds.

More affection and less resentment are helping Maureen and Jack relax into new levels of sexual pleasure, as well.

"At the tender age of seventy-four and seventy-six, we're finally getting there," says Maureen, "and it's so much fun!"

HOW ANGER CAN ENHANCE
A MARRIAGE

Jack and Maureen's experience shows the good changes that can happen when couples learn to accept anger and use it as a catalyst for improving their marriage.

One key is to recognize anger as a positive emotion. In fact, images from brain scans show that we experience anger on the left side of the brain, along with feelings of amusement and intense interest. Unlike sadness or fear—which are experienced on the right side of the brain and cause us to withdraw from the world—anger can stir us to engage with others, to take action, and to get involved.

Like all emotions, there's a logic and purpose to anger. We typically get angry when we see injustice, believe we've been treated unfairly, or encounter an obstacle to achieving our goals. If we can learn to use anger constructively, it can inspire us to make positive changes on our own behalf—to try harder, to fight for what's fair, and to communicate more passionately. We can use anger to *italicize* our language so that other people can hear and understand how strongly we feel about an issue. And, as Jack and Maureen learned, we can use anger to improve our relationships.

For anger to be useful, however, you must be willing to express it and respond to it openly. And that can be a real challenge, especially if you experience anger as frightening, destructive, or out of control. From this perspective, anger may seem like a snowball of thoughts and feelings that gathers more strength and power as it goes downhill. (Example: "How could he treat me that way? He must think I'm some kind of loser, an idiot . . . That makes me so furious I could just fly off the handle . . . Who knows what might happen? I'll show him who's a loser . . .") A cascade of angry thoughts like this gives way to feelings of more shame, more fear, and more intense anger, until the emotions feel like an avalanche, threatening to destroy everything in its path.

If you typically lose control of your anger in this way—or fear that you might—you may benefit from counseling that can help you to rewrite the script. With assistance, you may learn to perceive anger as a logical, legitimate experience that can be managed and that can lead to improved conditions in your life. (Example: "I feel angry because of the way he treated me . . . I have a right to feel this way . . . It makes sense to have these feelings . . . I really need to be heard here . . . I can handle this feeling . . . If I speak up now, I can fix this situation and make it better . . . ") When you can experience anger as a positive, constructive force in your life, you may no longer feel as if you have to keep your anger hidden all the time. You learn to express it, so that others can better understand your experience, which leads to less resentment and a better chance at problem solving.

In marriage, couples may improve their relationship by reacting to each other's anger with this same kind of respect. If you approach your partner's anger with the idea that there's a logical, legitimate reason behind his or her feelings, then you may be able to use that anger as a resource for improving your marriage.

The secret is to help your partner understand the source of his or her anger. Asking simple, open-ended questions without trying to change your partner's feelings may be useful. Such questions might be "Why are you angry?" "You seem so frustrated right now. Tell me what's going on." "What do you need right now?" "What do you wish would happen in this situation?" (See more questions in the exercise on pages 216–17.)

But what if you feel that your spouse's anger is aimed directly at you? Well, that's a challenge, for sure. The angry partner needs to do his or her part by expressing feelings in ways that avoid contempt, hostility, or blaming. They need to focus on their own needs rather than their partner's faults or deficiencies. This allows the partner who's listening to feel less defensive, more willing to be influenced. The two of you will be less likely to fall into patterns of attack/defend/counterattack.

The importance of having somebody listen to you when you're angry can't be overstated. Years ago, psychologists believed that if people would just express their anger—"get it off their chests," so to speak—they could "get over" being angry and their lives would improve. This idea of being able to banish anger as though it were as simple as relieving a pressure valve has since been proven wrong. In fact, psychologists have found that simply venting your anger—i.e., ranting or raging without the benefit of an understanding listener—just makes you *angrier*. What you need when you're angry is empathy. You need somebody to listen and to say, "I care about what you're going through, and I want to understand." Having a receptive listener helps you to accept your angry feelings, work through them, and calm down.

Of course, it's hard for people to listen and to be understanding and caring when they're under attack. So take care to express anger in ways that are constructive and respectful—especially when the person you're most angry with is your spouse. The section titled "Healthy Complaining Versus Harmful Complaining" in chapter 1 may help.

A Special Message for Husbands: "Embrace Her Anger"

We believe that either partner's anger—expressed and understood—can be a resource for improvement in marriage. But our research shows this is especially true for women's anger. That's why one of the most powerful messages we give to husbands is this: "Embrace your wife's anger." Pay attention to it and follow it to its source. That's where you're likely to find the keys to making your marriage better.

We believe this message is especially pertinent today because women are now being educated and empowered to achieve more economically, politically, and socially. But our culture still teaches that women who assert themselves to get what they want are being "pushy" or obnoxious. Women who get angry when their goals are blocked are labeled "bitchy" or rude.

"Nice ladies," as Maureen told Jack, may feel angry, but many don't express their anger—especially not in the company of men. Consequently, these same "nice ladies" are often frustrated and misunderstood. They feel disrespected and resentful toward the men in their lives, and that resentment snuffs out feelings of appreciation, affection, passion, and romance. Meanwhile, their anger "leaks out" at inopportune moments—in the middle of a church discussion group, for instance.

Where does this leave a man like Jack, who would like to have a more loving relationship with his wife, but feels bewildered or upset by her chilly responses or angry outbursts? We believe he can make tremendous progress toward greater intimacy in his marriage by tapping into his wife's anger and helping her to say what's on her mind. This can be done by asking her questions when she's angry, and showing concern about the things that make her mad. To do so shows that he cares about what she's feeling, what her goals and aspirations are, and what's getting in the way of those desires. By doing so, he proves that her perspective really matters to him. He becomes her confidant and her ally.

Aretha Franklin had it right when she sang, "R-E-S-P-E-C-T—*find out what it means to me.*" Embracing your wife's anger means showing her your respect. And, as Aretha demonstrates, "just a little bit" can go a long way toward unleashing feelings of appreciation, affection, passion, and romance.

Quiz: How Do You Feel About Anger?

The following quiz can help you and your spouse compare your attitudes about expressing anger.

As you read each question, think about recent episodes when you or your spouse felt angry. If you're not absolutely sure how to answer, that's OK. Just indicate the answer toward which you more or less lean.

PARTNER A   **PARTNER B**

T/F   T/F

____   1. I am either calm or I blow up in anger; there's not much in between.   ____

____   2. I can tell when I'm starting to get angry because I feel a little grumpy or irritated.   ____

____   3. I think it's best to keep my angry feelings to myself.   ____

____   4. My view is that if you suppress anger, you're courting disaster.   ____

____   5. Anger is usually inappropriate.   ____

____   6. Getting angry makes me feel more powerful, as if I'm standing up for myself.   ____

____   7. For me, anger is a time bomb waiting to explode.   ____

____   8. Anger gives you drive.   ____

____   9. I think getting angry is uncivilized.   ____

____   10. For me, anger and getting hurt go together; when I'm angry, it's usually because I've been hurt.   ____

____   11. I don't see the difference between anger and aggression.   ____

____   12. It's hard for me to sit still when I'm angry.   ____

____   13. I think people should pay the consequences for angry outbursts.   ____

____   14. When I get angry, people know they can't just push me around.   ____

____   15. I cope with my anger by letting time pass.   ____

____   16. Getting angry feels like blowing off steam, letting go of pressure.   ____

____   17. Anger is OK as long as it's controlled.   ____

____   18. For me, anger is a natural reaction, like clearing your throat.   ____

____   19. When people get angry, it's as if they're dumping their garbage on other people.   ____

PARTNER A   PARTNER B

T/F   T/F

____   20. I think that if you always try to hide your anger, it will make   ____
            you sick.

____   21. Anger is like fire; you've got to stop it right away, or it will   ____
            consume you.

____   22. Anger gives me energy; it motivates me to tackle problems   ____
            and not be defeated by them.

SCORING: Add one point for each even-numbered item (2, 4, 6, 8, etc.) that you answered "true." Subtract one point for each odd-numbered (1, 3, 5, 7, etc.) item that you answered "true." The higher your score, the more comfortable you are with anger.

If you and your spouse have substantially different scores, you may have lots of conflict about the way anger is expressed in your marriage. The following exercise may help you to reconcile some of that conflict.

Exercise: When You and Your Partner Have Different Ideas About Anger

Partners' attitudes about expressing anger may differ widely based on their experiences with anger as a child or experiences that may have occurred in their adult lives when they let their anger show. If you and your spouse find yourselves at odds over this issue, it's usually best to discuss your feelings about anger directly. The following steps can help:

1. Take the quiz on the previous pages and discuss how each of you answered each item.

2. Take turns answering the following questions about your individual histories with the emotion of anger:

- How did you feel as a child when your father became angry with you? With your mother?

- How did you feel as a child when your mother became angry with you? With your father?

- What significant things have happened in your life when you have become angry at some person, situation, or thing?

3. As you and your partner answer these questions, try to understand how your life experiences with anger may differ. Despite those differences, express understanding toward your partner if you can.

4. See if you can arrive at an agreement about expressing anger in your marriage that honors both of your points of view. Some compromise may be necessary. The following exercise may help.

Exercise: Responding to Anger in a Helpful Way

Anger often comes up when somebody's got a goal, but they're feeling blocked or frustrated in their attempts to achieve it. Sometimes that person might not even know what their goal is. They just know they're angry and they'd like to feel better. The first step may be to figure out what the goal is. Then you can figure out what's getting in the way and what to do about it.

On page 217 are some questions to help with that process. You can use them by yourself when you're feeling angry. Or you can use them as a starting point for a conversation with your spouse when he or she is mad.

If you decide to use them with an angry spouse, remember this rule: *Understanding must come before advice.* In other words, it's better to let your partner get all his or her feelings out and for you to try to understand those feelings, before you begin problem solving or exploring what to do.

Also, if the conversation gets so intense that one or both of you start to flood (that is, your heart rate soars and you can't think clearly), you may need to take a break and set a time to come back to the conversation. (See the exercise in chapter 2, "Calm Down to Avoid Flooding.")

- What are you angry about?

- What are your goals in this situation?

- What are your needs here?

- What do you want to see happen?

- What are you trying to accomplish?

- What does this issue mean to you?

- What are all your feelings about this situation?

- What is so frustrating for you in this situation?

- What do you see as the obstacles to getting what you want?

- What's standing in your way?

- What's painful about this situation?

- Is there something about this that seems unfair?

- Is there something about this that seems immoral or wrong?

- What have you tried to do in the past?

- Has that worked before?

- If so, can you do it again? If not, why not?

- What could you do differently this time?

- What are some other things that you can think of doing to accomplish this same goal?

- How can I help you?

CHAPTER 9

"We Only Have Time for the Kids Now"

Like many parents of small children, Ron and Melissa look back at their childless years together and marvel at all the time they once had to just relax. As newlyweds living near Cincinnati, Ron was in business school while Melissa taught art classes at a community college. At the end of the day, they would meet in their kitchen and swap stories.

"Ron loves to cook," Melissa explains. "So I would watch and we would yak while he made the meal."

"We always ate dinner late because it took a long time to prepare," he remembers. "Then, afterwards, we would just sit for the longest time and just talk."

All that changed when Ron and Melissa became parents after eight years of marriage. Now, when Ron comes home from his job as a manager at a software company, he's greeted at the door by their two sons, Alex, age four, and Collin, ten months. Melissa, now a stay-at-home mom, is often exhausted by 6:00 p.m., and she's ready for Ron to take the kids off her hands.

"I feel like it's crunch time as soon as I walk in the door," Ron complains. "There are too many things happening all at once. Alex wants my attention.

218

I need to change my clothes. I need to get dinner made . . ."

"I usually cook these days," Melissa responds, and Ron nods in agreement, falling silent, looking sad. It's obvious that their long, intimate dinners are a thing of the past.

All told, Ron and Melissa say they're a "great team" when it comes to meeting their kids' needs. "But sometimes I feel like that's all we are," says Ron, forty-two.

Take bedtime, for example. Melissa, thirty-six, feels strongly that babies should not sleep alone. So, for the time being, Collin has a place in his parents' bed. The trouble is, the baby often doesn't rest well near Melissa; he keeps trying to nurse throughout the night. So, lately, Melissa's been leaving him in the bed with Ron and going off to the guest room to sleep by herself. Consequently, the couple finds very little time for cuddling with each other. Sex at night is out of the question.

As for the rest of the day, Melissa says there's never enough time or energy to relate to each other as lovers. "We want to be connected that way, but I'm always afraid that if I tell Ron, 'I

What's the Problem?

- Ron and Melissa focus totally on their kids' needs, while ignoring their emotional and sexual needs as a couple.

- Melissa feels lonely, isolated from Ron, so she pursues his attention.

- Ron feels criticized, incompetent in Melissa's eyes, so he withdraws.

- Neither partner clearly states needs.

- Neither partner has a blueprint for handling conflict.

What's the Solution?

- Express your needs to each other in more specific ways.

- Turn toward each other's needs.

- Learn to use a blueprint for handling conflict.

- Make your marriage the top priority, recognizing how this will benefit the kids.

feel lonely,' or suggest that we do something together, he'll respond with, 'Sure, Melissa. But when are we going to find the time?' "

Ron and Melissa describe their relationship as a kind of pursuit: Melissa's always pressing Ron for more attention and more help, and Ron is perpetually pulling away. Our research shows that this dynamic—where the wife persistently seeks help and attention from a retreating husband—is common among couples adjusting to parenthood.

"He communicates with me, but it's almost grudgingly," she says. "He'll complain, 'You're so intense, Melissa!' And I'm like, 'Yeah, that's because you're not here!' I don't like being intense. But I want you to notice me!"

"What does 'intense' mean to you?" John asks.

"It means she's always getting in my space with some immediate demand," says Ron.

"Yeah, I *want* to be 'in your space!' " says Melissa, exasperated. "That's the problem."

"But I always end up feeling like I've failed you before I even get the chance to respond," says Ron.

To hear more, we ask Ron and Melissa to discuss a recent conflict. They zero in on a tense moment that happened while preparing dinner the night before.

What They Say	What We Notice
Ron: I think I make assumptions when I read your body language. It's this vibe that you're impatient with me—disapproving. Like last night, when we were getting ready for dinner, I was crouched down at the refrigerator and you tried to give me the baby.	+ Takes responsibility as he describes the problem. +/− Tries to avoid blaming, but slightly critical.

What They Say	What We Notice
Melissa: Oh, right.	+ Shows she's listening, nondefensive.
Ron: I was putting stuff into the back of the fridge, and all of a sudden there's this baby hovering over my head. And I'm thinking to myself, "Would you give me five seconds to do this before I have to grab the baby? Just back off that much!" I get this feeling that I've done something wrong. I feel like I'm being slow or stupid.	+/− Describes his frustration, but slipping into accusation. + Good description of feelings.
Melissa: The feeling of impatience is hard for you?	+ Good question.
Ron: Yeah, because it seems very disapproving. And I don't . . .	− Blaming.
Melissa: I think it's that I'm desperate. I have less patience now than I would like to have. And I feel that I talk more than you want me to. It's like you're thinking, "I've heard it all. You're repeating yourself." So now I try to talk less. I don't talk when I probably should. Like I should say, "Ron, I can't carry a crying baby around and do what I need to do. Would you hold him, please?"	− Interrupts. + Expresses her feelings. − Assumes she knows what he's thinking ("mind reading"). + Takes responsibility for her part of the conflict.
Ron: Right.	+ Shows he's listening.

continued

What They Say	What We Notice
Melissa: And if I said that, then you wouldn't be so surprised. *Maybe. (Sarcastic tone.)* You wouldn't feel like I was so impatient because there would be warning with words.	+/– Takes responsibility, but her sarcasm shows contempt.
Ron: Ummhmm. The problem is the way I read you. It just gets me into trouble all the time.	+ Still listening, admits that his "mind reading" is a problem.
Melissa: Well, yeah. Because you think I'm angry and I'm not. And then you get angry because you think I'm angry.	+ Good insight.
Ron: I'm thinking, "Why is she pissed at me?"	+ He validates her insight.
Melissa: See, we're misinterpreting each other! It doesn't come across to me as "Why is she pissed at me?" It comes across as "She's pissed, so now I'm pissed!" And then I *am* pissed. I get upset because you're angry at me and I don't know *why* you're angry at me. You're angry at me because you think I'm angry at you.	+ More good insight about how their fights escalate when they make assumptions, don't state their feelings. + Expresses feelings.
Ron: Right.	+ Validates.
Melissa: It's a lose-lose situation. And being stuck about sex—it feels the same way. I don't know how to get out of the loop we're in.	+/– More good insight, but could say more about how she feels.

What They Say	What We Notice
Ron: I don't, either.	+ Validates.
Melissa: I fantasize. I wrote on the anniversary card I gave you, "Let's practice falling in love again." That's really what I'd like. I'd like us to both go, "OK. We're going to have an attitude change for a week." To just have a test period where you would think, "Now, I'm going to think that Melissa thinks I'm brilliant and sexy and prepared."	+ Starts to share her feelings. + States what she needs.
Ron: Until the next time I'm not.	+ Reveals his feelings of inadequacy in her eyes.
Melissa *(impatiently)*: No! No! No, not until the next time you're not. Just to try that attitude.	+/− Clarifies her need, but tone is critical.
Ron: Ummhmm. *(Long silence.)*	+/− Indicates he's listening, but doesn't tell her how he feels.
Melissa: So when did it change between us? Why did it change?	+/− Question shows willingness to go deeper; but "why" may result in intellectualizing, when what they really need is to share immediate feelings.
Ron: I don't know. That's a good question.	+ Shows responsiveness.
Melissa: Because if it had been like this fifteen years ago, we wouldn't be together now.	− Critical.
Ron: I guess it's a result of having had the same arguments a number of times. Having that same feeling of "Here we go again."	+ Good insight.

Our Analysis: Focus on the Kids Disguises the Real Trouble—Failure at Expressing Needs

Ron is right. Recurring dead-end arguments can lead to a sense of hopelessness, and that's not good for a marriage. Still, we see embers of hope in Ron and Melissa's relationship. We notice, for example, that both partners listen carefully to each other and respond in ways that are nondefensive. They're proud of the "teamwork" they share in caring for their children, and their devotion to their kids motivates them to look for solutions to the difficulties they're facing as a couple.

At the same time, they're quite frustrated. Like many couples adjusting to life with children, they tend to attribute many of their problems to their role as parents. They tell themselves that they're so busy meeting the kids' needs, there's no room to think about their needs as a couple. But as we've learned in our research, meeting your kids' needs and meeting your spouse's needs are not mutually exclusive goals. In fact, the best thing you can do for your child is to take good care of your marriage—and that's where we find Ron and Melissa struggling.

One problem is the way they express their needs to each other. For example, Melissa tells Ron that she wants to "practice falling in love again." But it's not clear to him how they're supposed to do this. Meanwhile, he seems quite anxious at the prospect of letting Melissa down. Exploring his family history, we learn that when Ron was a young teenager, his parents divorced and his mother left the family. It's not unusual for children of divorce to experience a sense of grief and helplessness at their inability to keep their families intact. In fact, Ron tells us he feels he was "always disappointing" his mother.

"This childhood experience may contribute to a sense of discomfort with Melissa's emotional intensity," John tells Ron. "It leaves you feeling no matter what you do, it won't be good enough," says John.

So when Melissa complains that she's "lonely" or "desperate" for his help—but then doesn't communicate what would make her feel better—Ron feels destined for failure. Faced with the prospect of disappointing Melissa, he withdraws. Poised to believe that he can't do right by his wife, he often reads more into her irritation or frustration than is warranted. Meanwhile, Melissa becomes frustrated by Ron's reaction and complains more intensely, causing Ron to become even more discouraged, to retreat even further.

Our Advice

Ron and Melissa need to do a better job of identifying and expressing their needs to each other. When Melissa feels she needs Ron's help, attention, or affection, she should tell him, *in precise ways,* what she's looking for. By using specific words or actions, she gives Ron a chance to help her feel understood, comforted, nurtured, attractive, and loved. (Examples: "I need you to hold me." "I need to set a date for dinner— just the two of us." "I need you to tell me I'm pretty." See the exercise "Give Me a Clue" on pages 235–36 for more.)

In addition, Ron needs to tell Melissa how she can help him to feel more accepted and competent in her eyes. Would it help, for example, for Melissa to acknowledge when Ron responds to her requests? What would it mean to him for Melissa to say that she appreciates how he paid attention, made the effort, and got it right?

We also suggest that Ron try some new responses when he feels uncomfortable with Melissa's demands. For example, rather than retreating from her intensity, he might say, "I'm afraid I'm going to let you down again, and that's not acceptable to me. I want to meet your needs. So tell me specifically: What do you want in this situation? What do you need right now?"

"Couples don't do this very much," John tells them. Instead, they simply engage in a kind of competition of self-sacrifice. "One partner will say, 'You don't get your needs met in this relationship? Well, I don't get my needs met, either!' But imagine what would happen if partners responded, 'You don't get your needs met? That's wrong! Both of us should be satisfied in this relationship, so let's figure out how to make that happen.' "

And finally, we suggest that Ron and Melissa use the "Blueprint for

Handling Conflict" that's described on pages 241–42. We believe this exercise can be especially helpful for them because of Ron's tendency to withdraw when Melissa's complaints become emotionally intense. The blueprint provides a way to stick with the discussion, build understanding, and arrive at compromise.

In this next conversation, we suggest that Ron and Melissa try to clearly tell each other what they need from this relationship.

What They Say	What We Notice
Melissa: I'm trying to figure out how to make our relationship a priority—along with meeting the parenting needs and work needs. Because I often hear, "There's no time for being physically close." But there *is* time for reading a book or working on a project, or something else.	+/− Boldly addresses the issues, but doesn't tell him how she feels about it.
Ron: Ummhmm.	+ Shows he's listening.
Melissa: And I think it would be good to spend some time being physically closer to each other. If I were to say, "I need to feel attractive to you," or "I need you to feel like I am attracted to you," what do we do about that? How do we . . . ?	+/− Gets close to addressing her needs, but focuses on how to "solve the problem" rather than how she feels about it.
Ron: I think we have to do a lot more things in passing. Like having a phone conversation. Or just squeezing it in between cooking and sitting down to dinner. Maybe some of the touching will happen if we just try to do things in little instants.	+/− Shows willingness to work with her, but he, too, is focused on the "how-to" rather than on his feelings.

What They Say	What We Notice
Melissa: OK.	+ Validates, accepts what he's saying.
Ron: Like if I just come by and give you a hug and keep on going. If we can make that more of a habit, I think that would be really nice.	+ Starts to address his feelings, what he feels would be "nice."
Melissa: I think we could have held hands when we were walking during lunch today. *(Long silence.)* I guess it's scary. I'm scared of jumping off this bridge after not being physically in touch for a while.	+ Expresses her disappointment. + Expresses her fear.
Ron: Ummhmm.	+/− Listening, but not really drawing her out with questions.
Melissa: And I'm thinking that you perceive being physically in touch as being sexually in touch.	+/− Expresses her fears, although in an analytical way, which can take her away from feelings.
Ron: OK.	+ Listening.
Melissa: You say that I don't like it when you touch me. And, yeah, when you grab my butt when Alex is there, that doesn't feel appropriate to me. But holding hands or a hug or something—that feels more like it. Then we could be in touch without it being intimidating.	+ Starts describing her feelings. + Expresses her needs for affection.
Ron: Sure.	+ Accepts what she's saying.

continued

What They Say	What We Notice
Melissa: When we're not in touch that way, having you grab my butt feels sort of crass.	+/− More feelings, starting to criticize.
Ron: OK.	+ Accepts.
Melissa: Like it's not coming from someplace loving.	− More criticism.
Ron: So you don't want me to do that when Alex is in the room. And you don't want me to do that when we're feeling out of touch.	+ Shows he understands.
Melissa: I need to start more gently than that.	+ Clarifies.
Ron: I agree.	+ Accepts.
Melissa: What do you need? Or what are you feeling right now?	+ Good questions.
Ron: Well, I think I need to feel comfortable touching you.	+ States his need.
Melissa: I'd like you to feel comfortable touching me. When you don't touch me, I feel pretty bad.	+ Validates his needs. + Expresses her feelings.
Ron: Ummhmm.	+ Listening.

What They Say	What We Notice
Melissa: And you're distancing yourself for some reason. I don't know why you're not comfortable.	− Criticizes him.
Ron: Often when I kiss you, you don't look in my eyes and I'm not sure why.	+ Gives information.
Melissa: I didn't know that.	+ Takes it in.
Ron: And last night before we went to bed you were in the middle room . . .	+ Gives her a specific example.
Melissa: Oh yeah, I was sort of looking around.	+ Goes along with him.
Ron: You were looking at a catalog. Then you got up to brush your teeth and I was kind of following you around and I really just wanted to kiss you. And I think I finally caught up with you on your way back into the room. And you just sort of said, "Good night." And I really felt brushed off.	+ Expresses specific need. + Expresses feeling.
Melissa: And I felt really sad.	+ Expresses feeling.
Ron: Huh.	+ Takes it in.
Melissa: I felt really sad and really lonely. The whole time.	+ Expresses feeling.

continued

What They Say	What We Notice
Ron: Hmm. Interesting.	+ Listening.
Melissa: And I would have loved to hear, "I want to kiss you good night." Or, "Can we snuggle?" That would have felt great for me.	+ Expresses specific need and longing.
Ron: OK. I just need to tell you more.	+ Accepts what she's saying.
Melissa: Or you could say, "What do you need?" or "How are you feeling?" That would be great.	+ Working it out, telling him what she needs.
Ron: Good. I can do that.	+ Accepting her influence.
Melissa: Yeah. We could figure out a way to not feel lonely. I could figure out a way to feel close to you.	+ Expressing approval, acceptance, hope.

This conversation has taken Ron and Melissa into new territory—a place where they're bravely talking about feelings and needs that were previously cloaked in tension and silence. This is not an easy conversation for them, but as they demonstrate, it gives them a sense of hope that their marriage can improve.

Before closing, we encourage both partners—but Ron especially—to keep asking questions and reflecting back the answers they hear. This may encourage Melissa to be more specific in stating her needs. Then he'll have the information he needs to prove to her that he's listening and willing to meet her needs.

We also encourage them to make their relationship the number-one priority in their lives for at least the next year. This sounds challenging, especially considering their commitment to being great parents. But we remind them that improving their marriage is probably the best thing they can do for their children's well-being.

And finally we remind them that putting their marriage first means that each spouse is willing to do more than his or her fair share. "Don't worry if things seem out of balance—if it feels like you're giving more than fifty percent to this partnership," says John. "That's the way it has to be for a while." If Melissa says she needs help with the kids, Ron needs to drop everything and be there, John advises. If Ron needs reassurance that he's appreciated, Melissa should provide that reassurance without condition. Acting this way could build a new foundation of trust, appreciation, and affection. If that happens, they'll be reaping the rewards for many years to come.

Two Months Later

Ron and Melissa say they accepted our advice about communicating their needs—and it's had good results. They've agreed, for example, that when one person wants something, all they have to do is say so. "We can just say, 'This is what I need, and I need it now,'" Ron explains. "And the other person will respond without a lot of questions or delay."

This agreement has taken much of the tension out of their day-to-day lives together, the couple reports. Each partner is spending less emotional energy wondering, "Is it OK to ask?" or "Do I deserve this?" Whether the request involves help with a crying child, a hug when feeling lonely, or time to sit down and hash out a problem, the answer is the same: "Here I am." The results are warmer feelings and more spontaneity. And with less tension and hesitation in their interactions, they've having sex more often.

In addition, Ron and Melissa are making more time for guilt-free, individual pleasures. For example, Melissa is taking a yoga class twice a week. Ron is planning a week-long hiking trip with a friend. These activities require lots of cooperation around child care and household chores. But they're also a way for the partners to say, "I really care about you and your happiness—so go. Do something nice for yourself. I've got it covered."

What's Wrong with a Child-Centered Marriage?

For couples intensely committed to being good parents, having a "child-centered marriage" may not sound like such a bad thing. After all, kids need and deserve an enormous amount of attention from their moms and dads. Problems arise, however, when couples use their parenting obligations as an excuse for neglecting their relationship with each other.

In a child-centered marriage, kids can become the great distraction—a convenient way to ignore your need for adult conversation or romance, or to sidestep marital problems that ought to be addressed. Examples of child-centered couples might include:

- *the pair who points to a child's sleep patterns as the reason they've stopped having sex*

- *the partners who say that between Little League, Scouts, and science projects, there's absolutely no time for that weekend getaway*

- *the couple that claims that the husband's job must be the primary focus of his life because the family needs a substantial income to send the kids to the best colleges*

Do you see the pattern? The couple's needs are always trumped in favor of the kids'. But in the long run, the children's needs aren't really being served at all. Parents who feel they missed important experiences or necessities in their own upbringing may be at special risk for having a child-centered marriage. These parents may be so focused on "getting it right" for their own offspring that *everything* else—including their marriage—takes a backseat to their children's needs. The sad irony is that in striving to create the perfect life for their children, these parents fail to provide what kids need most—a happy home. Spouses who neglect the health of their marriage may inadvertently create an environment that's rife with tension and susceptible to downward spirals of defensiveness, criticism, contempt, and stonewalling.

Our research has shown that growing up in a strife-filled environment can have a strong negative impact on children's attitudes and achievements. Children who live with unspoken tension in the family may become anxious, depressed, introverted, and withdrawn. Children who live with hostility and contempt become aggressive with their peers.

On the other hand, parents who take good care of the marriage—who listen and respond to each other's needs—provide their kids with great role models for healthy relationships. They also create a relaxed, happy environment where kids can thrive physically, emotionally, and intellectually. In our workshops with new parents, we often encourage couples to think of their marriage as they would a cradle. It's here in the safety of your stable, loving relationship that your child's heart can rest. Keeping that cradle strong and peaceful is the best thing you can do to ensure your child's long-term well-being.

To determine whether yours is a child-centered marriage, take the following quiz. For more advice on prioritizing family needs, see the section in chapter 3 "How a Little Selfishness Can Help Your Marriage."

Quiz: Is Your Marriage Child Centered?

Answer the following questions:

PARTNER A   PARTNER B

T/F   T/F

____   1. I often find myself disappointed in this relationship.   ____

____   2. I have learned to expect less from my partner.   ____

____   3. It's hard for my deepest feelings to get much attention in   ____
this relationship.

____   4. I feel as though our life together is one long list of errands   ____
we have to do.

____   5. I feel as if I can't do anything right.   ____

____   6. I often feel criticized by my partner.   ____

____   7. There is not much intimacy in this relationship right now.   ____

____   8. Our great conversations have somehow vanished.   ____

____   9. Sometimes our relationship feels empty to me.   ____

____   10. I don't feel very important to my partner anymore.   ____

____   11. We are now separate and unconnected emotionally.   ____

____   12. We don't really talk very deeply with each other.   ____

____   13. There's not enough closeness between us.   ____

____   14. The children take up all of our energy.   ____

____   15. My partner seems to have lost interest in me.   ____

____   16. I don't feel that my partner is very attracted to me these   ____
days.

____   17. There's certainly not much romance or passion in this   ____
relationship.

____   18. I can't really say that we are very good friends right now.   ____

____   19. I am lonely in this relationship.   ____

SCORING: If you answered "true" on six or more of the items above, you and your spouse need to put more focus on your relationship as a couple in order to recognize each other's needs and to turn toward bids for connection. The following exercises may help.

234

Exercise: Give Me a Clue

What would you say if your partner asked, "What do you need from me in this marriage?" Perhaps you'd answer, "I need to feel loved," or "I need to feel respected." But would your spouse know what to do in order to help you feel that way?

This exercise may help you and your partner determine specific actions each of you can take to meet the other's needs. The idea is to eliminate the need for guesswork or "mind reading." Partners no longer need to feel "clueless" when responding to each other as friends, confidants, and lovers.

The instructions are simple. Read the examples below. Then get two sheets of blank paper. Each of you should write down five things (feelings, values, ideals) that you need from the relationship. Then, for each need, give three examples of actions your partner could take to help you fulfill that need. Then take turns sharing what you've written.

Tip: Try to state your needs in positive ways rather than as complaints. For example, don't say, "You never tell me what happens at work." Say, "I'd like to hear more about your job."

Examples:

WHAT I NEED: I need to feel loved.

Three actions my partner can take that would help me feel this way:

1. Touch me in an affectionate way. (Hold my hand when we walk down the street, put your arm around me in a crowd, snuggle close when we're watching TV.)
2. Make a date to spend time alone with me.
3. Do small, thoughtful favors for me. (Pour me a cup of coffee, offer to run an errand for me, cook my breakfast once in a while.)

WHAT I NEED: I need to feel that you're my friend.

Three actions my partner can take that would help me feel this way:

1. Take my side in an argument.
2. Invite me to do things with you.
3. Agree to see the movie I want to see sometimes.

WHAT I NEED: I need to feel sexy.

Three actions my partner can take that would help me feel this way:

1. Touch me this way (then demonstrate).
2. Kiss me out of the blue.
3. Tell me when I do something that excites you.

WHAT I NEED: I need to feel appreciated.

Three actions my partner can take that would help me feel this way:

1. Say thank you when I do things for you. (Cook dinner, get the car washed, pay the bills.)
2. Say nice things about me in front of other people.
3. Plan a dinner for my birthday.

WHAT I NEED: I need to feel respected.

Three actions my partner can take that would help me feel this way:

1. Listen when I tell you my opinion of the news.
2. Be on time to pick me up.
3. Try my suggestion for fixing something.

Exercise: Turning Toward Your Partner's Bids for Connection

We believe Melissa and Ron can improve their marriage by clearly telling each other what they need in terms of acceptance, friendship, affection, and romance.

Imagine, for example, what might have happened on that lonely night they describe on page 229 if either one had made a clear bid for emotional connection. What if either Ron or Melissa had said, "I really want to kiss you right now"? And what if the other had responded, "That's what I really want, too"?

Our research has shown that such exchanges are the stuff that happy marriages are made of. Whether a partner wants sex, affection, conversation, or just some help with the yard work, the story is the same: One partner makes a bid in the form of a comment, a gesture, a question, a touch, or a facial expression. And the other partner "turns toward" that bid with interest, empathy, or support.

While turning toward your partner's bids leads to the growth and development of a loving, caring relationship, "turning away" by ignoring your partner's bids has just the opposite effect. Whether the slight is intentional or simply caused by mindlessness, continually disregarding your partner's bids leads to increased conflict, hurt feelings, and the deterioration of your relationship.

"Turning against" your partner's bids with arguments and hostility also has a negative impact. It can make the bidding partner feel hurt and fearful, so that bidding stops, feelings are suppressed, and the relationship begins to wither.

Below is a list of situations in which partners commonly bid for emotional connection. As you read each item, imagine your partner offering this bid to you. Then imagine ways that you might turn away, turn against, or turn toward the bid. Over the next several weeks, see what happens when you make an effort to habitually turn toward your partner.

Examples:

BID: My partner pours me a cup of coffee as I'm working at the computer.

Turning-away response: Silence. No acknowledgment.

Turning-against response: "Looks like you made it too weak again."

Turning-toward response: "Thanks. That's so thoughtful."

BID: My partner reads aloud a joke that he or she thinks is funny.

Turning-away response: "Have you seen my black shoes?"

Turning-against response: "I can't concentrate when you're reading like that."

Turning-toward response: "That's funny." Or "I don't get it. Tell me why it cracks you up."

BID: My partner tells me some bit of news about a relative.

Turning-away response: _____

Turning-against response: _____

Turning-toward response: _____

BID: My partner mentions something that needs to be done in the yard.

Turning-away response: _____

Turning-against response: _____

Turning-toward response: _____

BID: My partner tells me we're out of laundry detergent.

Turning-away response: _____

Turning-against response: _____

Turning-toward response: _____

BID: My partner admires the neighbor's new car.

Turning-away response: _____

Turning-against response: _____

Turning-toward response: _____

BID: My partner touches me in an affectionate way.

Turning-away response: _____

Turning-against response: _____

Turning-toward response: _____

BID: My partner complains about a chronic health problem.

Turning-away response: _____

Turning-against response: _____

Turning-toward response: _____

BID: My partner says he or she is worried about our child.

Turning-away response: _____

Turning-against response: _____

Turning-toward response: _____

BID: My partner touches me in a way that usually leads to sex.

Turning-away response: _____

Turning-against response: _____

Turning-toward response: _____

BID: My partner tells me he or she is very tired.

Turning-away response: _____

Turning-against response: _____

Turning-toward response: _____

BID: My partner recalls something from childhood that was very hurtful.

Turning-away response: _____

Turning-against response: _____

Turning-toward response: _____

BID: My partner tells me about an incident at work where he or she felt unfairly treated.

Turning-away response: _____

Turning-against response: _____

Turning-toward response: _____

Busting the Myth of Spontaneity in Romance

"No time for sex and romance" is one of the most common complaints we hear from parents. The problem, they say, stems from nonstop, immediate demands of caring for young children. Once the kids arrive, it feels as if your entire life is booked. When you're not at work, you're running errands, doing housework, or caring for the brood. You feel that you have no privacy. And if you get around to having sex at all, it's usually at the end of the day when both of you are exhausted. For many tired parents, making love often feels like "the last chore of the day."

That's why we heartily recommend that couples schedule regular "dates"—evenings or weekends when you get a babysitter so you can have time alone together to keep romance alive in your relationship.

"But scheduling sex and romance takes all the spontaneity out of it," we hear couples complain. "That's no fun." We contend that such thoughts are a big mistake. To understand why, think about the most romantic times in your relationship. If you're like most people, you'll be remembering those first few dates. Now think back to how you used to get ready for those times together. You may remember preparations that were anything but spontaneous. In fact, people in new romantic relationships are often thinking far ahead, with considerations such as, how will I dress? What perfume will I wear? Should I dim the lights? How will I make my moves? And, most of all, how will all this feel? Did all the preparation take the fun out the relationship? Hardly. Instead, it added fuel to the sense of anticipation and excitement for the evening ahead.

So we advise couples to get their calendars out and start planning. Set aside some time and then use your imaginations to plan for romance, plan for sensuality, and plan for sex.

If, for whatever reason, planning for sex causes one or both partners to suffer "performance anxiety"—that is, to fear that they won't fulfill their partner's needs or expectations for the date, that's OK. The key is to talk to each other about those fears and offer reassurance. Then together you can take your expectations down a notch and focus on simply experiencing relaxation and pleasure together. Plan time for activities like hot baths, back rubs, touching, holding, and simply making each other feel good physically and emotionally. If sex happens, that's fine. But if it doesn't, you'll still have met your expectation of enjoying time together.

Exercise: A Blueprint for Handling Conflict

Some people avoid conflict because they fear getting hurt or hurting their partners. In fact, some know from experience that arguments with their partners *always* end up that way; the two start to disagree, the disagreement escalates and then "blows up." Meanwhile, nothing gets resolved.

If that's your experience, the following exercise may help. Based on the ideas of social theorist Anatol Rappaport, we developed this exercise as a structure or "blueprint" for couples to use in talking about their differences.

Step 1. Set aside a quiet time to discuss one single conflict at length.

Step 2. Designate one person as the speaker and one person as the listener.

Step 3. The speaker begins talking about the conflict, saying everything they want to say about their point of view. The listener can ask questions and take notes. Writing things down gives the speaker the distinct feeling that what they're saying really matters to the listener—and that's the point of the exercise.

When the listener asks questions, those questions are simply to ensure understanding. *The listener must delay talking about solutions and postpone any attempt to try to persuade the speaker.* The listener can't use questions to imply he or she disagrees. The listener should

not present his or her own views. The listener can't correct the partner's facts or express reactions to the speaker's view. The listener's
job is simply *to listen.* The whole interaction should be civil and
polite.

Step 4. When the speaker is completely finished, the listener restates the speaker's point of view. The speaker listens carefully and
clarifies anything the listener didn't really seem to grasp. Then the
listener restates the position. This process repeats until the speaker
is satisfied that the listener really understands.

Step 5. Switch roles and start over with Step 1.

Once you've completed these steps, you or your partner have not yet
persuaded each other to see things differently. You may still have con-
flicting points of view. The exercise postpones persuasion until each
person can state the partner's entire point of view to the partner's satisfaction. Then, and only then, can persuasion begin. You may now discuss your differences and try to compromise, or you may still "agree to
disagree." Either way, however, it's likely that each of you will feel
heard and better understood. In that state, you feel more emotionally
connected to your partner, and that makes for a stronger marriage.

CHAPTER 10

"You're Not Satisfied Unless There's Some Drama"

Terry was attracted to Amanda the first time he saw her entering the kitchen in the Austin restaurant where they both worked. But she let him know early on that she wasn't interested.

"I told him I didn't go out with coworkers," the former waitress remembers. "And besides, I was more inclined to date wild, long-haired drummers in rock bands."

This clean-cut law student, who was working part-time as a cook, didn't fit the mold. But a few weeks later, when he invited her to join him hiking in the Hill Country, she consented.

"He was taking his dog, and I just love dogs, so I decided to go," explains Amanda, now thirty-five. Soon she found herself sitting next to him on a rock, thinking, "Wow, I'd really like to kiss him!"

She resisted the impulse—for about six hours. But by the end of the day, she wasn't limiting herself to drummers anymore. And by the end of the year, they'd moved in together.

Nine years later, Terry looks back to those early days as "a real roller-coaster ride." He blames the turmoil on the old saw "opposites attract." That is, the qualities they found most attractive in each other were the very things that drove them apart. While Amanda was outgoing,

What's the Problem?

- *Terry and Amanda have many "perpetual issues"—ongoing conflicts based on differences in personality and preferred lifestyle.*

- *When Amanda states her feelings about a conflict, he backs away.*

- *To avoid conflict, Amanda backs away, too.*

- *Habitual retreat from feelings creates emotional distance.*

- *Emotional distance contributes to physical distance.*

What's the Solution?

- *Quit avoiding conflict.*

- *Seek dialogue over perpetual issues.*

- *Communicate acceptance of each other's personalities; appreciation that "opposites attract."*

- *Take time alone together to rebuild emotional and physical intimacy.*

Terry was more introverted. While Terry strived for stability, Amanda was looking for excitement, taking risks.

"Her friends would party all weekend long, doing all kinds of crazy stuff," Terry, now thirty-seven, remembers. "Amanda liked the chaos of that scene, but I wasn't comfortable with it."

Amanda was often unhappy because she wanted their lives to be "more glamorous," says Terry. But Amanda says their problems actually centered on her longing for autonomy. "Terry was the stronger, more solid person in our relationship and I always felt like I was being subsumed into him," she explains. "I really resisted that."

She moved out several times, but invariably she'd return. "I couldn't go for more than two or three days before I really missed him and felt like I just need to touch base," she says. "So then I'd come back. He was my best friend."

After four years of ups and downs, Amanda had a conversation with her mom that changed everything. "I was telling her, 'Terry's a nice guy, but I don't think I want to be with him forever.' And my mom nice guy, but I don't think I want to be with him forever.' And my mom said, 'OK, young lady—then you break up with him right now and leave him for good!' Her words just shocked me and I started to cry. I said, 'God, no. I can't imagine my life without him.' But she said, 'Well, that's where you'll end up if you keep doing what you're doing.' "

A year later, Terry and Amanda were wed.

By the time they visit the Love Lab, they've been married nearly four years, their daughter Danielle is two years old, and their second baby is on the way. Terry has a job with a prominent Austin law firm. Amanda is working part-time as a corporate trainer.

Although they've been generally happy, both complain that they don't feel as close emotionally or physically as they'd like to. In addition, they're continually struggling with a host of problems we call "perpetual issues"—that is, fundamental differences in personality or lifestyle preference that repeatedly create conflict.

"She's always dreaming up things for us to do that would be dramatic shifts in our life," says Terry. "Things like moving to Costa Rica or joining the Peace Corps. Last week she thought we should become organic farmers. And I'm thinking, 'Where does this stuff come from?' "

"I just have a certain level of adrenaline that needs to be channeled into something exciting," explains Amanda.

"And that tendency drives me crazy," Terry complains. "I very much want things to be comfortable. It's not that I'm totally averse to change . . ."

"But I'm totally averse to calm," Amanda laughs.

Conflicts over finances also continue. "I'm somewhat conservative financially," says Terry, "but I don't always communicate the plans that I have."

"So when he wants to spend money on something I think is frivolous, he says we have the money," Amanda explains. "But when I want to spend money on something, all of a sudden he says, 'We can't afford that right now.' "

Whatever the conflict (money, friends, lifestyle), if Amanda keeps pressing an issue, "Terry just tenses up and gets real quiet," she says.

245

"I don't like conflict very much," he admits. "I don't even want to talk about it."

Still, he and Amanda both know they've got to keep talking about important issues if they're going to bridge the gap that's growing in their relationship—a gap that's starting to affect their sexual relationship as well.

"It's impossible for me to be sexually aroused when I am not emotionally engaged," explains Amanda. "Foreplay for me is deep conversation."

To get a better picture of how they approach perpetually difficult issues, we ask them to try discussing a current hot topic. They decide to talk about money and how to manage it during Amanda's upcoming maternity leave. Here's an excerpt of that conversation:

What They Say	What We Notice
Amanda: We haven't had much time to sit and plan because we've had so much going on.	+ Shares responsibility for the problem of not planning.
Terry: Ummhmm.	+ Shows he's listening.
Amanda: Which is why I keep feeling so anxious, but then I feel sort of silly—like I'm making a big deal out of it when I know there are all these other things that . . .	+/− Describes her feelings, but then discounts them.
Terry: Right. I feel if I've got time to sit and talk, then I've got time to get other stuff done.	−/+ Interrupts, but validates what she's saying. + States his priorities.

What They Say	What We Notice
Amanda: Yeah. And we're getting to this place where we really do need to make the communication a priority. But I know there is all the landscaping stuff and the house stuff. I've tried on a couple of occasions to set up times for us to have to talk about things.	+ States her real need: to communicate. + Expresses frustration, without blaming.
Terry: Have you?	+ Shows he hears her; asking for a reminder.
Amanda: Well, that's why Mary took Danielle. That was supposedly what we were going to do.	+ Shares information.
Terry: I don't recall we got to that.	+ Shares responsibility.
Amanda: No, we didn't. *(She laughs nervously.)* I think you ended up having the softball game.	+/− Tries to keep it light, but slightly blaming.
Terry: That's right. And then I went out to the pub with the team.	+ Acknowledges responsibility for the problem.
Amanda: And I went out with Mary and Danielle for a while. I mean, it was my fault, too. But now I'm feeling that need to follow you around and say, "Hey, what's our plan here?" And I'm having a hard time.	+ Shares responsibility. + Expresses her need, worries.

continued

What They Say	What We Notice
Terry: And I'm concerned because I've got that case coming up in San Antonio. That's kind of a rush, rush, high-stress engagement for me.	+/− Expresses his need, but doesn't acknowledge hers.
Amanda: Yeah.	+ Validates, shows she's OK with his work.
Terry: I mean, I'll have three hours in the car each day.	− Slightly defensive.
Amanda (kidding): Maybe I should just go with you and we could talk in the car. (She laughs at her own joke.) That would be fun.	+ Makes a joke to keep it light.
Terry (smiling): Yeah.	+ Accepts the joke.
Amanda: I mean, I'm getting really kind of scared about the whole thing. Like last night when I thought I might be in labor, it was just kind of scary. Because we haven't really had a chance to talk about . . .	+ Expresses more feelings.
Terry: We need a couple more weeks.	− Avoids focusing on her feelings.
Amanda: And I'm starting to get that feeling of wanting to jump in front of your face and go, "We're going to have this baby very soon!" And it's like you don't have time to talk. That's not a priority.	+ Expresses feelings, but in a more intense way. − Slightly blaming.

What They Say	What We Notice
Terry: You said you were not going to go back to work until September. Is that right?	+/− Finally focuses on her, but zeroes in on her work schedule rather than her feelings.
Amanda: Well, I don't know. I feel really uncomfortable with the idea of leaving a newborn in day care.	+ More feelings.
Terry: Yeah, I'd just as soon you take as long as we can afford.	+ Shows support for her emotionally.
Amanda: I just wasn't sure if we could afford that. I don't want to end up with the same situation we had after Danielle was born. I felt that because I wasn't bringing in a paycheck, I didn't have any authority over any expenditures. Even though I was working harder than I'd ever worked in my life. And yet you get really tense about where we are financially and you make remarks when I need some money transferred into my account.	+ Expresses more fears, going deeper.
Terry: What for?	− Ignores her feelings, focusing on the spending instead.

continued

What They Say	What We Notice
Amanda: You'd say, "You figure out where the money's going to come from, because I don't know." And I don't know what the problem is. Because just a month ago, you were buying wine and fancy yard equipment. When you're making expenditures like that, I'm thinking, "Huh? Well, I guess we're doing pretty good!"	— Blames, attacks.
Terry: We were doing fine (nervous laughter).	— Tries to deflect her feelings.
Amanda: Until the stock market crashed (smile).	— Goes along with him, backing away from her own concerns and feelings.

Our Analysis: Perpetual Issues Lead to Conflict Avoidance, Lack of Connection

The smiles and laughter in this conversation point to a great strength in Terry and Amanda's marriage—their genuine feelings of warmth and affection for each other. This brings a sense of "we-ness" to the relationship. They both seem willing to share responsibility for their problems. And while there's a little bit of blaming going on, we don't see a lot of defensiveness. That's another strength. Also, when the conversation gets tense, Amanda is quick to offer repairs in the form of soothing remarks, punctuated with a joke or a smile, which Terry accepts. This kind of interaction keeps the tone of their conversation friendly and productive.

So why, if there's so much warmth and good humor in this relationship, are they feeling increasingly isolated from each other emotionally and physically? A closer look at the dialogue reveals some subtle clues.

Notice that each time Amanda talks about her feelings, Terry tends to back away. For example, when she says she's worried about their lack of planning around finances for her maternity leave, he responds by asking her for concrete information about her work schedule. And when she talks about her fear of having no money of her own after the baby arrives, he asks her why she needed money when their first child was small.

To his credit, Terry's questions probe issues related to the topics Amanda brings up. This shows he's interested in what she's saying. But he doesn't seem comfortable grappling with the emotions she's expressing. His words fall short of letting her know that he understands her fears and worries, empathizes with her, and would like to offer reassurance. In fact, if you were to look at his words alone, it would be hard to determine whether he and Amanda share anything more than a joint checking account and babysitting duties.

Terry is not alone in his avoidance. Each time he sidetracks the conversation, Amanda goes right along with him—perhaps out of fear of losing the connection altogether. In this way, they remind us of David and Candace in chapter 2—the couple who were so afraid of trouble after recovering from David's extramarital affair that they sidestepped every conflict that came their way. And perhaps the turmoil in Terry and Amanda's early relationship has had the same effect on them.

The trouble with avoiding conflict, of course, is that it can cause a gulf in the relationship to grow. This may be particularly hazardous for couples like Terry and Amanda, who have such basic personality differences—and therefore so many perpetual conflicts. Habitually trying to sidestep all these issues leads to emotional distance. And for Amanda, especially, that lack of emotional connection leads to a lack of interest in sex, romance, and passion.

Our Advice

Rather than avoiding conflict, Terry and Amanda should take a careful look at their goals around their differences. We're not suggesting that they try to find the perfect solution to their disagreements over money, friends, lifestyle, and so on. Obviously there's no single true answer to the kinds of perpetual differences this couple faces. Amanda is a planner, Terry is not. Terry likes solitude, Amanda would rather party. Amanda likes lots of change, Terry likes things to stay stable. Neither partner is "right" or "wrong" in these desires. So the best approach is to simply *establish a dialogue* about the conflict—to be able to talk about your disagreements on an ongoing basis and still feel good about each other. The idea is to "make peace" with your differences, realizing that a happy coexistence will require lots of compromise, lots of give-and-take ahead.

It also helps to realize that your perspective on your partner's personality is just that—one person's perspective. In fact, Terry and Amanda tell us that in their own families of origin, Terry was considered quite "wild" compared to his brothers. And Amanda was "the stable, practical one" among her siblings.

We advise Terry and Amanda to try viewing their conflict as they would a third party outside the relationship—a project that the two of them are going to keep working at in a collaborative way. "The problem is *not* your partner," John says. "The problem isn't this 'money thing' or this 'planning thing' over which you disagree. That problem is like a soccer ball that the two of you are kicking around. You work together, looking at it together from different angles, figuring out how to get it down the field. Sometimes you make progress in your discussions and sometimes you don't. But you learn to live with it and don't let it harm your relationship."

The most important thing is to avoid getting "gridlocked" in your positions, he adds. To become gridlocked is like being in a bumper-to-bumper traffic jam; there is no movement, no compromise. You feel stuck and eventually you begin to see each other as enemies on either side of the issue. Remember, you don't have to be adversaries just because you hold opposite points of view. As Terry stated early on, "opposites attract"—and for good reason. When opposites are willing to see the world from the other person's perspective, they get to see the whole picture, and that can be a terrific advantage for couples.

Recognizing that you can talk about your conflicts without harming the relationship is also a great advantage in terms of building emotional intimacy—which is just what Terry and Amanda need to do. So in their next conversation, we advise them to go further into their feelings about a perpetual issue, focusing this time on *accepting* each other's differences. This time they discuss another long-standing conflict—their disagreement over the best place to live.

What They Say	What We Notice
Amanda: I think I'm fearful sometimes that, left up to you, we would just never . . .	+ States her fear.
Terry: We'd stay in the same house.	+ Shows he understands.
Amanda *(laughing)*: We'd be in the same house. And it's not that I'm unhappy there, but I feel like there's much that I want to do and experience.	+ Softens her complaint with laughter. + Goes deeper into feelings, needs.
Terry: Well, I agree that we need to do as much as we can, but you know how I feel about throwing everything out of the window and starting over. I'm well down the road in my career and I'm afraid of changing the course too much.	+ Validates her need. + Expresses his own fear.
Amanda: Ummhmm.	+ Shows she's listening.

continued

What They Say	What We Notice
Terry: I wish I could be more like you. I wish I could embrace change, because it would make our life more interesting, I'm sure.	+ Expresses appreciation for her personality.
Amanda: I'd like to be more like you, because it would make me a little more comfortable, but . . .	+ Expresses appreciation back.
Terry: But we're not going to change each other.	+ States acceptance of their differences.
Amanda: No.	+ She agrees.
Terry: So we have to be happy living together.	+ States shared goal of happiness.
Amanda *(laughing)*: Or split up.	+ Keeps it light with humor.
Terry laughs.	+ Accepts her joke.
Amanda: My worst fear is that I'm ultimately going to have to make a decision between . . .	+ Goes further into feelings.
Terry: Well, let's talk specifics. We've always had this idea that we're going to move on to a different house after a few more years.	− Interrupts her at a crucial point to avoid going deeper.

What They Say	What We Notice
Amanda: And I was thinking three years . . .	− Goes with his train of thought, allowing him to take her away from expressing her feelings.
Terry: Why would we have ever bought a house if we were thinking of moving in just three years?	− Interrupts her again; domineering.
Amanda: Because that's the amount of time it takes before you would consider . . .	+ Responds with information.
Terry: Yeah, but I don't like to think about that.	− Interrupts her again; domineering.
Amanda: Don't you see how I have compromised in this situation to better fit your lifestyle? And for the most part, I'm fine with that. I certainly wouldn't go back and do it any differently if it meant not having our children.	+ Expresses her frustration, resentment. +/− Reassures him that she values the relationship, but holds back a bit.
Terry: But what if it just meant not having me?	+ Reveals fear of losing her; asks for reassurance.
Amanda: Oh, that's all part of the package.	+ Offers some reassurance.
Terry: But it's separate.	+ Keeps pressing for the reassurance he needs.
Amanda: No, I wouldn't do it differently if it meant not having you.	+ Gives him the complete reassurance he needs. *continued*

What They Say	What We Notice
Terry: Good. That's nice to hear.	+ Expresses his relief, gratitude.
(They pause as Amanda laughs. Then they sit for a moment, just smiling at each other.)	+ Express warmth and affection.
Terry: When we do move, where do we go?	+ Now he's ready to go along with her; asks for her ideas.
Amanda: Well . . .	+ Starts to respond.
Terry: Let's say I'm in the same job, so we stay in Austin. You don't like the suburbs.	− Interrupts her. + Acknowledges her preferences.
Amanda: No. I like the idea of living further out. You could set up a satellite office.	+ Agrees and expresses her feelings; problem solving.
Terry: Maybe. But what about your more recent ideas of just throwing away everything that we have?	+/− Expresses his fears, although in an exaggerated way.
(She frowns.)	+ Protests his exaggeration.
Terry: I don't mean that you . . .	+ Recognizes her distress and tries to repair.
Amanda: I think that's what you hear when I talk.	+ Expresses her feeling that he's being unfair.

256

What They Say	What We Notice
Terry: Well, when you say you want to move to Costa Rica, that's kind of what I hear. OK?	− Slightly defensive. + Expresses his fear.
Amanda: I'm saying Costa Rica to stress what I don't like in our current lifestyle. And sometimes I feel like you don't value things that I find increasingly important in terms of the way that we're raising our family. You know, being around all this commercialism and seeing our children influenced by all this stuff.	+ Expresses her feelings. − Blaming. + Expresses her worries.
Terry: I share your concerns, but I don't share your solutions.	+ Validates her worries. + Clarifies the conflict.
Amanda: But we need to get a break. To get a year away from all the noise and all the commercials and all the ugliness.	+/− Expresses her needs; tries to convince him, but she's stopped telling him how she feels.
Terry: I just don't think we're in a position where we can coast. Maybe in ten years we can do something like that. But I'm afraid to say, "Yeah, that sounds like a great idea," because you'll just go and do it.	− Resisting, not communicating. + Finally expresses his feelings.
Amanda: When you say that, I feel like you don't trust me. Like I've done all these terrible things in the past. But I've never done anything that led us to ruin.	+ Expresses how hurt she feels when he becomes so resistant.

continued

What They Say	What We Notice
Terry: No. *(Pauses, smiling.)* Thanks to me.	+ Repairs the interaction with a smile and humor.
Amanda *(laughing)*: I mean, I'm a risk taker, yeah.	+ Accepts the repair; lightens up. + Acknowledges his point of view; accepts their differences.
Terry: *(Laughs, smiles at her with absolute adoration.)* Yes, you are. That's one of the things I like about you.	+ Expresses affection, love, acceptance. + Validates her personality.
Amanda: I have all this energy about having adventures and experiencing life. And it keeps getting tamped down until I get these crazy thoughts of just driving off into the sunset—just to see what would happen. Do you understand where I'm coming from?	+ Expresses feelings. + Asks for his understanding, acceptance.
Terry: Yes, I do. I do.	+ Extends his understanding, acceptance.

"This was an extremely productive conversation," John tells Terry and Amanda. "Not that it was fun or easy—you were talking about some tough issues. But you shared a lot of humor, affection, and respect for each other."

Most important, they were no longer ducking the tough issues. "Terry, you were talking about what you really fear and what you really need," John adds.

Amanda agrees. "It was definitely helpful to hear Terry say, 'I want the same things you do, but I'm afraid.' When he says that, I don't feel that we're on opposite sides anymore."

In addition, Terry and Amanda have openly acknowledged that their conflict is based on personality traits that they love in each other. Terry wishes he could "embrace change" like Amanda does. Later on, when he talks about what a "live wire" his daughter Danielle is, he just beams. It's clear that the little girl takes after her lively, adventurous mother, and that's what Terry loves in both of them. By the same token, Amanda says she wishes she could be more like Terry; she can see the merits of calmly settling down into this comfortable life they're building.

"I call this a 'delicious conflict' because it's bigger than just the conflict between the two of you," says John. "It's about a conflict that each of you carries *within yourselves.*"

Therefore, the more Terry and Amanda seek to understand each other, the more they'll each grow as individuals, John explains. "As long as you keep talking to each other this way, your conflicts are going to enrich your lives rather than drive you apart."

We offer Terry and Amanda a few more pointers. First, Terry needs to be aware of his tendency to interrupt Amanda—especially when he's feeling anxious. We notice that this domineering behavior results in Amanda shutting down and then fantasizing about getting away. Our advice? Be sure that Amanda has plenty of freedom to express herself in the relationship. Don't cut her off. Listen to what she's saying.

We also encourage them to keep expressing their appreciation and gratitude for the lives they're building together. (See the "Thanksgiving Checklist" on pages 268–270.) Doing so will warm the environment for more romance and intimacy.

And finally, as we do with all couples with small children, we strongly urge them to take time in their lives for sex and romance. (See the section in chapter 9 titled "Busting the Myth of Spontaneity in Romance.")

Two Years Later

When we check back with Terry and Amanda two years later, we find out that Terry has made partner in his law firm—a change that guarantees they'll stay in Austin for quite some time. In fact, they're still living in the same house—the one that Amanda felt certain they would have sold years ago.

Does all this stability still bother Amanda? "Not as much as it used to," she says. Maybe that's because she's had a few adventures on her own in recent years. For example, she and Danielle recently took a trip to Costa Rica as part of a cultural exchange program Amanda helped to organize through their church.

Still, Terry says he expects Amanda's restlessness to reemerge as a source of conflict in the future. "Maybe not this year or the next—but soon she'll feel she's in a rut and she'll shake things up somehow," he predicts.

"Our struggles are always changing and evolving," Amanda adds. "As soon as we get something resolved and put it behind us, we come to a place where we're facing some deeper struggle. In fact, sometimes I'm afraid that we're just working ourselves up to the mother of all marital conflicts."

At the same time, both partners say they're growing more confident in their ability to handle their conflicts as the years go by.

"We've certainly had our up and downs, both before we got married and after," says Terry. "I don't know what the next set of problems is going to be, but after all we've experienced, I'm pretty confident that we're going to get through them."

DON'T GET GRIDLOCKED OVER
PERPETUAL ISSUES

Every marriage has perpetual issues—that is, conflicts based on personality differences or preferences in lifestyle that never go away. Common examples include disagreements over spending, where to live, or how to handle household chores. Our research shows that the happiest couples can live peacefully with their perpetual issues as long as they keep talking about them in an open, productive way. However, perpetual issues that become gridlocked conflicts can be harmful to a marriage.

In gridlocked conflict, couples

- *express little amusement or affection when they discuss the problem*

- *take the issue very personally, and feel rejected by each other when it comes up*

- *make each other "villains" in the conflict; one partner is completely right and the other is completely wrong*

- *become entrenched in their positions, never compromising*

- *spin their wheels, digging themselves deeper and deeper into conflict*

- *eventually become emotionally distant, disengaged*

To keep a perpetual issue from becoming gridlocked, you can

- *make dialogue your goal rather than finding the perfect solution*

- *see the problem as a third party outside your relationship; the problem is not your partner*

- *recognize that there are no "right" and "wrong" solutions*

- *accept that the conflict may never go away, but you can live together peacefully anyway*

- *look for humor in conflict*

Quiz: What Are Your Perpetual Issues and What Are Your Gridlocked Problems?

Every marriage has perpetual issues—those conflicts that just keep recurring, no matter what. But just because the same conflict keeps popping up again doesn't mean it has to harm your marriage.

Below is a list of common perpetual issues. There's also room at the bottom to fill in some of your own issues if they're not listed here.

In the first column, circle the issues that ring true for you and your partner. Then, looking back at each of the issues you've circled, ask, "Can my partner and I can still talk about this issue and find ways to compromise? Or are we gridlocked?" Make a check mark in the second or third columns as appropriate.

Is this issue a source of a perpetual conflict in your marriage	If so, do you talk and compromise?	Or do you gridlock?
1. Neatness and organization Partner A: Thinks it's important to be neat. Partner B: Doesn't think neatness matters that much.		
2. Emotional expression Partner A: Explores emotions and expresses them freely. Partner B: Is less comfortable with expressing or talking about feelings.		
3. Independence versus togetherness Partner A: Wants to spend more time together, to be more dependent on each other.		

Is this issue a source of a perpetual conflict in your marriage	If so, do you talk and compromise?	Or do you gridlock?
Partner B: Wants more time apart, to have more autonomy.		
4. Frequency of sex		
Partner A: Wants sex more often.		
Partner B: Wants sex less often.		
5. Sex and emotional intimacy		
Partner A: Wants to feel emotionally close before initiating sex.		
Partner B: Wants to have sex as a way to get emotionally close.		
6. Finances		
Partner A: Spends carefully, tries to save.		
Partner B: Spends freely, saves less.		
7. Family ties		
Partner A: Wants independence and distance from relatives.		
Partner B: Wants to spend time with and feel close to relatives.		
8. Household chores		
Partner A: Wants an equal division of labor.		
		continued

Is this issue a source of a perpetual conflict in your marriage	If so, do you talk and compromise?	Or do you gridlock?
Partner B: Does not want an equal division of labor.		
9. Disciplining children		
Partner A: Is stricter with the children.		
Partner B: Is more permissive with the children.		
10. Being on time		
Partner A: Thinks it's important to be on time.		
Partner B: Thinks being on time is no big deal.		
11. Socializing		
Partner A: Is extroverted, wants to spend more time with other people.		
Partner B: Is introverted, would rather spend time alone or as a couple.		
12. Religion		
Partner A: Places more value on religious practice.		
Partner B: Places less value on religious practice.		

Is this issue a source of a perpetual conflict in your marriage	If so, do you talk and compromise?	Or do you gridlock?
13. Ambition Partner A: Is more interested in success at work. Partner B: Is less interested in success at work.		
14. Romance and passion Partner A: Wants more romance and passion in life. Partner B: Doesn't care that much about romance and passion.		
15. Adventure Partner A: Wants more adventure and excitement in life. Partner B: Doesn't care that much about adventure; thinks life is exciting enough.		
16. Perpetual issue _____ Partner A: _____ Partner B: _____		
17. Perpetual issue _____ Partner A: _____ Partner B: _____		
18. Perpetual issue _____ Partner A: _____ Partner B: _____		*continued*

Is this issue a source of a perpetual conflict in your marriage	If so, do you talk and compromise?	Or do you gridlock?
19. Perpetual issue _____ Partner A: _____ Partner B: _____		
20. Perpetual issue _____ Partner A: _____ Partner B: _____		

As you review your check marks in the second column, consider how you and your partner can keep your minds and hearts open to each other around this issue. How can you keep talking, keep compromising, and keep stretching to find common ground?

As you review the check marks in the third column, consider whether there's any room for new dialogue or compromise on this issue. If you come up blank, look back at the section in Chapter 5 titled "Your Hidden Dreams and Aspirations: The 'Prairie Dogs' of Marital Conflict." As the material in this chapter explains, gaining a better understanding of each other's hopes and dreams is often the best way to break through gridlock.

Exercise: Creating a Culture of Shared Values and Meaning

Like Terry and Amanda, many couples are attracted to each other by their "opposite" natures. While this can be the basis of a vibrant marriage, it also requires lots of sensitivity and vigilance as you learn to accept and honor each other's points of view. By doing so, you create a culture of shared values and meaning in your marriage. This isn't something that happens automatically or overnight. Rather, it's a process that occurs as partners find ways to live side by side, respecting each other's goals, dreams, and perspectives. This exercise is a series of questions designed to encourage that process.

We recommend that partners each get a personal notebook. Then select one or two questions from the list that you'd like to think about. Write down your answer to the question. Then share what you've written with your partner. Discuss your answers, looking for areas of common ground, agreements you can build upon. Talk about your differences as well, finding ways to honor values and philosophies that both of you hold.

Some of these questions are big enough to stimulate hours of conversation, so don't feel that you need to tackle these questions all at once. In fact, you may want to come back to these pages time after time, selecting just a few questions that seem most important to you at various phases of your life.

- *What goals do you have in life, for yourself, for our marriage, for our children? What would you like to accomplish in the next five to ten years?*

- *What is one of your life dreams that you would like to fulfill before you die?*

- *We often fill our days with activities that demand immediate attention. But are you putting off activities that are great sources of energy and pleasure in your life? What are those activities?*

- *Who are we as a family in the world? What does it mean to be a _____ (insert your family's last name)?*

- *What stories from your family history are important to you?*

- *What does the idea of "home" mean to you? What qualities must it have? How is this like or unlike the home where you grew up?*

- *How important is spirituality or religion in your life? How important is it in our marriage and in our home? How is this like or unlike the home where you grew up?*

- *What's your philosophy of how to lead a meaningful life? How are you practicing (or not practicing) this philosophy?*

- *What rituals are important to you around mealtimes?*

- *What rituals are important to you around holidays?*

- *What rituals are important to you around various times of day (getting up, leaving the home, coming home, bedtime, etc.)?*

- *What rituals are important when somebody in our family is sick?*

- *How do we each get refreshed and renewed? How do we relax?*

- *What rituals do we have around vacations?*

- *What does it mean to be to be a husband or a wife in this family?*

- *What does it mean to be a mother or a father in this family?*

- *How do you feel about your role as a worker?*

- *How do you feel about your role as a friend? As a relative? As a member of our community?*

- *How do we balance the various roles we play in life?*

Exercise: Thanksgiving Checklist

We have learned that couples rarely improve their marriages by trying to change each other. Rather, partners find happiness by focusing on each other's positive attributes. Expressing gratitude and appreciation for these qualities creates a loving, accepting atmosphere between you—an optimal environment for building understanding around perpetual issues and finding ways to compromise.

For this exercise, take turns selecting three items from the following list that you really like about your spouse. (You can add your own items if you'd like.) Tell your spouse which three items you've selected for him or her. Describe in detail how you see these qualities expressed, and talk about the way they make your life better. Then thank your spouse for being this way.

I am grateful for:

- your energy

- your strength

- the way you take charge

- the way you let me direct things

- how sensitive you are to me

- how you support me and respond to my needs

- your ability to read me

- how I feel about your skin

- how I feel about your face

- how I feel about your warmth

- how I feel about your enthusiasm

- how I feel about your hair

- the way you touch me

- how safe I feel with you

- how I feel about your tenderness

- how I feel about your imagination

- how I feel about your eyes

- the way you move

- how I can trust you

- how I feel about your passion

- how you know me

- how I feel about your gracefulness

- the way you kiss me

- your playfulness

- your competence as a spouse

- your competence as a parent

- your sense of humor

- your friendship

- your loyalty

- your sense of style

- _____

- _____

- _____

- _____

Index